KWAME N

THE STRUGGLE CONTINUES

Six panaf pamphlets

PANAF

© PANAF BOOKS LIMITED 1973

All rights reserved. No part of this publication may be reproduced, stored in a retrieval system or transmitted, in any form or by any means, electronic, mechanical, photocopying, recording or otherwise, without the prior permission of the publisher.

SBN 901787 41 8

Panaf Books
243 Regent Street
London W1R 8PN

Printed in the United Kingdom

Contents

WHAT I MEAN BY POSITIVE ACTION	5
THE STRUGGLE CONTINUES	
A Call to the Workers of Ghana	9
Message to the Black People of Britain	13
Africa Day Special Message	15
THE WAY OUT	
Ghana: The Way Out	19
"Civilian Rule" fraud	26
A Call for Positive Action and armed struggle	30
THE SPECTRE OF BLACK POWER	36
THE BIG LIE	45
TWO MYTHS	
The Myth of the "Third World"	74
"African Socialism" revisited	78

PUBLISHER'S NOTE

Each of the six pamphlets in this book was originally published separately. The first pamphlet, *What I Mean by Positive Action*, was written in 1949 at a crucial stage in the national liberation struggle in Ghana. In an atmosphere of mounting unrest particularly in Accra, Kwame Nkrumah was called upon by the Ga State Council to explain to members of his newly-formed Convention People's Party (CPP) what he meant by *positive action*. Working throughout the night, kneeling on the floor and using his bed as a table, he wrote *What I Mean by Positive Action*. In the statement he called for the use of non-violent methods in the anti-imperialist struggle believing rightly that in the circumstances of the time these tactics were likely to be the most effective. On the 8th of January 1950 he proclaimed the start of positive action with a general strike to begin at midnight. This led to his subsequent arrest and imprisonment by the colonial power, to be followed just over a year later by the victory of the CPP in a general election and his release from prison to form the first African government in a colonial territory.

The other five pamphlets were all written in Conakry, Guinea, between 1966 and 1968. They reflect the conclusions reached by Kwame Nkrumah towards the end of his life, on the various processes of the African Revolution and the world socialist revolutionary struggle. Emphasis is on class struggle, and the exposure of the close links between imperialists and neocolonialists and the indigenous bourgeoisie. While by no means ruling out non-violent methods, he is convinced of the need to employ all forms of struggle, including armed struggle, in order to complete the liberation of Africa and to bring about the unification of the continent under a socialist All-African Union Government.

What I Mean by Positive Action

Preamble: Party Members, Friends and Supporters

In our present vigorous struggle for Self-Government, nothing strikes so much terror into the hearts of the imperialists and their agents than the term *Positive Action*. This is especially so because of their fear of the masses responding to the call to apply this final form of resistance in case the British Government failed to grant us our freedom consequent on the publication of the Coussey Committee Report.

The term *Positive Action* has been erroneously and maliciously publicised no doubt, by the imperialists and their concealed agent-provocateurs and stooges. These political renegades, enemies of the Convention People's Party for that matter of Ghana's freedom, have diabolically publicised that the C.P.P.'s programme of positive action means riot, looting and disturbances, in a word violence. Accordingly, some citizens of Accra, including myself, were invited to a meeting of the Ga Native Authority and the Ga State Council on Thursday, October 20, at 1 p.m. "to discuss", as the invitation stated, "the unfortunate lawless elements in the country and any possible solution".

At that meeting, I had the unique opportunity of explaining what *Positive Action* means to the satisfaction of the Ga Native Authority and the Ga State Council, and the meeting concluded with a recommendation by them that I should call a meeting to explain to the members of the Convention People's Party as I did to them, what I mean by *Positive Action* in order to disabuse the minds of those who are going about misinterpreting the Positive Action Programme of the Convention People's Party.

Before I proceed to my proper topic, I must take this opportunity to dispel the wild rumour, that the Ga Manche said at the meeting that the Convention People's Party should be suppressed and that I should be deported from Accra. Nothing of the sort was ever suggested by the Ga Manche even though some of the speakers tried to convey such idea but the Ga Manche promptly overruled that.

And at this point allow me to protest vehemently against the diabolically false Reuters' news which no doubt must have been sent by their correspondent in this country. I read to you the text of the Reuters' news:

"Local African Chiefs have sent ultimatum to Extremist Home-Rule Leader Kwame Nkrumah demanding undertaking by next Wednesday not to cause trouble when Coussey Report on Constitutional Advancement of Gold Coast is published next week. He has also been told to promise Loyal co-operation of his Convention People's Party. If he refuses African Authority will 'Forcibly Eject' him from Accra to his Native Village of Nzima about 250 miles inland. All Political Leaders Promised co-operation in keeping peace except Dr. Nkrumah who said he had 'No Guns to Fight' but would resort to Boycott, Strikes and Spiritual Force to carry on struggle. Coussey Commission was set up last January to examine Proposals for Constitutional and Political Reforms in Gold Coast."

Party members, imagine the wicked misrepresentation, chicanery, falsehood, the untruths, the lies and deception, in such news. This is the way our struggle is being misrepresented to the outside world; but the truth shall ultimately prevail.

Why Positive Action?

It is a comforting fact to observe that we have cleared the major obstacle to the realisation of our national goal in that ideologically the people of this country and their Chiefs have accepted the idea of Self-government even now. With that major ideological victory achieved, what is left now is chiefly a question of strategy and the intensity and earnestness of our demand. The British Government and the people of Britain, with the exception of die-hard imperialists, acknowledge the legitimacy of our demand for Self-government. However, it is and must be by our own exertion and pressure that the British Government can relinquish its authority and hand over the control of affairs, that is, the Government to the people of this country and their chiefs.

There are two Ways to Achieve Self-government

There are two ways to achieve Self-government: either by armed revolution and violent overthrow of the existing regime, or by constitutional and legitimate non-violent methods. In other words, either by armed might or by moral pressure. For instance, Britain prevented the two German attempts to enslave her by armed might, while India liquidated British Imperialism there by moral pressure. We believe that we can achieve Self-government even now by constitutional means without resort to any violence.

We live by experience and by intelligent adaptation to our environment.

From our knowledge of the history of man, from our knowledge of colonial liberation movements, Freedom or Self-government has never been handed over to any colonial country on a silver platter. The United States, India, Burma, Ceylon and other erstwhile Colonial territories have had to wage a bitter and vigorous struggle to attain their freedom. Hence the decision by the Convention People's Party to adopt a programme of non-violent Positive Action to attain Self-government for the people of this country and their chiefs.

We have talked too much and pined too long over our disabilities—political, social and economic; and it is now time that we embarked on constitutional positive steps to achieve positive results. We must remember that because of the educational backwardness of the Colonial countries, the majority of the people of this country cannot read. There is only one thing they can understand and that is Action.

What is Positive Action?

By Positive Action we mean the adoption of all legitimate and constitutional means by which we can cripple the forces of imperialism in this country. The Weapons of Positive Action are:

(1) Legitimate political agitation:
(2) Newspaper and educational campaigns and
(3) as a last resort, the constitutional application of strikes, boycotts, and non-co-operation based on the principle of absolute non-violence.

How is Positive Action to be Applied?

We have been unduly criticised by our political opponents, that it is wrong for us to tell the imperialists that we shall resort to non-violent strikes and boycotts as a last resort, if need be, to attain our freedom. Their contention is that we should have kept this secret and spring a surprise on the Government. As for us, our faith in justice and fair play forbids us to adopt such sneaky methods.

In the first place, we like to use open methods and to be fair and above board in our dealings. We have nothing to hide from the British Government. Secondly, and what is more important if the C.P.P. is a democratic organisation, then the members must be taken into confidence and their approval secured for such an important policy, and they must be given the opportunity to prepare for any eventuality. Even, in the case of declaration of war, notice is first given.

Mr. C. V. H. Rao in his book entitled *Civil Disobedience Movement in India* has this to say.

"Constitutional agitation without effective sanction behind it of organised national determination to win freedom is generally lost on a country like Britain, which can appreciate only force or its moral equivalent ... An important contributory factor to the satisfactory settlement of a disputed issue is the extent and the nature of the moral force and public sympathy generated by the righteousness of the cause for which the suffering is undergone and the extent of the moral reaction it has produced on the party against which it is directed."

The passive sympathy of the masses must be converted into active participation in the struggle for freedom; there must also be created a widespread political consciousness and a sense of national self-respect. These can only be achieved when the mass of the people understand the issue. These are not the days when people follow leaders blindly.

When To Call Positive Action into Play

As already explained, Positive Action has already begun by our political education, by our newspapers agitation and platform speeches and also by the establishment of the Ghana Schools and Colleges as well as the fearless and legitimate activities of the C.P.P.

But as regards the final stage of Positive Action, *namely Nation-wide Non-violent Sit-down-at-home Strikes, Boycotts and Non-co-operation,* we shall not call them into play until all the avenues of our political endeavours of attaining Self-government have been closed. They will constitute the last resort. Accordingly, we shall first carefully study the Report of the Coussey Committee. If we find it favourable, we shall accept it and sing alleluya. But if we find it otherwise, we shall first put forward our own suggestions and proposals and upon refusal to comply with them, we shall invoke Positive Action straight away on the lines indicated above.

What we all want is Self-government so that we can govern ourselves in our own country. We have the natural, legitimate and inalienable right to decide for ourselves the sort of government we want and we cannot be forced against our will in accepting or perpetuating anything that will be detrimental to the true interests of the people of this country and their chiefs.

Therefore, whilst we are anxiously awaiting the Report of the Coussey Constitution Committee, I implore you all in the name of the Party to be calm but resolute. Let us advance fearlessly and courageously armed with the Party's programme of Positive Action based on the principle of absolute non-violence.

Long live the Convention People's Party. Long live the forward march of the people of this country. Long live the new Ghana that is to be.

A Call to the Workers of Ghana

WORKERS of Ghana; workers of our farms and peasant areas; workers in offices, factories and shops; workers in our Trade Unions; workers in the mines and railways; workers on the construction sites; workers in the public services; teachers and students in our schools, colleges and universities.

Since the 24th February, 1966, a little over two years ago, you have seen before your own eyes the degradation and shame which have been brought upon Ghana. Never before in our history has a clique of traitors betrayed the people and sold them to foreign interests. The so-called NLC with their neo-colonialist mentors and "domo"* cohorts sought political power by force, and by meaningless decrees are mismanaging and ruining Ghana.

You the workers of Ghana have a duty to perform, a duty stern and mandatory, to organise and to overthrow by force the clique of military-police puppets which calls itself the "National Liberation Council". A point has now been reached where you have no alternative. You have got to take a stand now and save Ghana.

Today, you the workers, farmers and peasants of Ghana, more than any others, know that Ghanaians are living under the grip of a neo-colonialist tyranny. The time is ripe for organised, aggressive action. It is time to organise the trade unions for a general strike simultaneously with a military counter-coup to overthrow the NLC and liberate Ghana from the clutches of neo-colonialism.

Consider the lot of the Ghanaian worker today; mass unemployment has hit the country, and the cost of living has soared to an unprecedented height. Thousands of those previously engaged in gainful employment today find it impossible to earn a living; hunger and crime plague the country.

Our free compulsory universal primary education and the free supply of text-books have been abolished. Many secondary schools have been closed down and welfare services stopped.

The Cedi has been devalued, and is soon to be devalued again. Ghana

---

* Ghana local nickname for local reactionaries, and refers to all opposed to the CPP.

is bankrupt. It is deception to announce wage increases amidst economic chaos and confusion; and wherever one looks at the tragedy it is the Ghanaian worker who has been hit hardest.

Meantime, the so-called NLC, in league with its neo-colonialist masters and local reactionaries, are busy forming private companies with themselves and their foreign manipulators becoming the directors on the boards of these companies.

American, West German and British private companies are sharing the booty of the exploitation of the Ghanaian people. This they call "Aid". The victimisation and humiliation of all those who advocate socialism as the African way of development still continues. How many commissions of inquiry will be needed to uncover the dark recesses of NLC corruption?

To conceal the truth, the NLC and their neo-colonialist masters embark upon campaigns of lies, propaganda and vilification, in order to divert the attention of the Ghanaian workers from the issues of hunger and exploitation and to destroy the will to overthrow them.

Their American "advisers" who have taken over the direction of their economic affairs are not in Ghana to seek solutions to our industrial and economic development but to squeeze out profits from Ghana. They have come to Ghana to ensure the exploitation of our country for the benefit of foreign capitalist interests.

In the past two years, by practical experience, you the workers of Ghana have come to know now what neo-colonialism is. The Ghana TUC which was built out of the sacrifices and struggles of thousands of our working men as an effective implement to better living conditions and to protect their industrial rights has been reduced to a disgraceful appendage of neo-colonialism.

Today, openly and shamelessly, the NLC has made our once glorious and dynamic Ghana TUC an apparatus of neo-colonialism. Where is the honour and dignity of our TUC in Africa today when John GORE of the American CIA employed by a so-called African-American Labour Centre sits in our former offices of the All-African Trade Union Federation (AATUF) as the principal of the so-called Ghana Labour College?

This is the extent to which the image and honour of our once glorious and invincible Trade Union Movement has been reduced by these neo-colonialist lackeys.

Why must the workers of Ghana sit and watch these things happen before their very eyes and yet do nothing about them? What will the founders of the Ghana trade union movement think of our generation? How can a movement with such fine traditions of struggle allow itself to be so denigrated?

Workers of Ghana, awake! This is the time to demonstrate your invincibility once more. We have not forgotten the historic role played by the Ghanaian TUC in the achievement of Ghana's independence. We have not forgotten the days when AATUF with its headquarters in Ghana was the hope and inspiration of other workers of Africa struggling for their freedom.

Where is our policy of non-alignment and the assertion of the African Personality in trade union affairs? How long are we going to continue to sit down unconcerned and see the name, honour and dignity of Ghana and the workers in particular dragged down, besmeared with mud?

All that which is right and reasonable pleads for action to avenge the honour and dignity of Ghana. To think or talk of constitutional formulas in the face of illegalities is to duck the truth and ignore realities. To attempt to argue or to listen to discussions, with the clique which has sold its conscience for a mess of pottage is criminal folly. To negotiate with renegades who have renounced their use of reason is to attempt the impossible.

The only language which is understood is force and action. Workers of Ghana reflect, take stock of events and deal with the present shameless situation with revolutionary firmness and zeal.

After a certain point the liberation struggle develops a continuity as a result of its past experiences. The Ghanaian worker must refuse to struggle under blackmail. The enemy has got its grip on our Achilles heel and we must kick back now or never.

Today we see before our own eyes the total and complete dismantling of the socialist sector of our economy. This sector built through sweat, toil and sacrifice for the welfare of the Ghanaian workers, is being handed over shamelessly to foreign capitalists.

The workers who in the past worked in our state hotels and felt the pride of working for themselves are today the employees of an American Hotel Corporation; many of them have been dismissed.

The free workers on our twenty-mile square State Rubber Plantation are today the slave labourers of the Firestone Rubber Company of America — a company known throughout the world for its oppressive labour policies: behold Liberia.

The breakdown of the economy of Ghana and the transforming of the country into a classic neo-colonialist client state must make the workers sit up, think and act. The institutions we built through years of hard work and socialist planning are being destroyed.

Our trade unions and militant workers must adopt Positive Action now to clear up the mess into which the country has been plunged. And this must take the form of countrywide co-ordinated Positive Action, not isolated protests. Once the fire is lit the blaze will spread throughout the country.

Workers of Ghana, arouse the anger of the people of Ghana into action! This is your total responsibility as a working class. If you put down your tools and refuse to work, if you stop production and stop making profits for foreign interests, if you organise yourselves and link up in Positive Action in the form of a general strike with other workers throughout the country you will have forced the NLC and their neo-colonialist manipulators to capitulate; you will have rescued our generation from complete political and economic disaster.

This is a sacrifice you must make. There is no other greater patriotic duty you could perform for Ghana. For the present generation of Ghanaians life can only spring up again out of the rotten corpse of the so-called NLC. The term "NLC" is a misnomer and has become symbolic — symbolic of degradation, shame and infamy.

But I know that there are a majority of the army and police, including officers, who would like to see Ghana freed from neo-colonialist control. These men are with us and are ready to join us in the march to action.

The task of the workers of Ghana now is direct action and struggle. Organise in your workplaces, in the mines, in the railways, at the harbours, on the construction sites, in public offices, in schools, colleges and universities.

Link up your resistance and Positive Action activities with the CPP in the wards, villages and in the countryside. The Party is emerging, born anew from its setback, fully tested and experienced to fulfil its historic role as the Party of the workers, farmers and peasants of Ghana.

Those who had remained in the ranks of the Party in the past for the purpose of amassing wealth and with no conviction in its socialist goals have been swept away by their own opportunism and misdeeds, and by their betrayal of the people's trust.

As I have said elsewhere, the slate has been wiped clean and the Party is emerging ideologically seasoned to continue the revolutionary struggle with the oppressed of Ghana, Africa and the world.

Workers, farmers and peasants in all parts of Ghana, organise and act now. You have to liberate your country once again as you did in the days of British colonialism. Your goal is historic—it is the building of a society in Ghana within a united socialist Africa.

Workers, farmers and peasants of Ghana do not despair or fear the future. Act NOW. The struggle continues.

Message to the Black People of Britain

MEMBERS of the Black Panther Movement and all my Black Brothers and Sisters, comrades and friends from the Caribbean, Africa, Asia, Latin America and all corners of the socialist world.

Greetings:

History rarely moves in a straight line; its course is uneven. Today as a result of the contradictions in capitalism, neo-colonialism and racism, Black Power is emerging on the stage of history. The oppressed of the earth are seeking a new way out to resolve these contradictions and achieve total emancipation.

What is Black Power? By Black Power we mean the power of the four-fifths of the world population which has been systematically damned into a state of undevelopment by colonialism and neo-colonialism. In other words, Black Power is the sum total of the economic, cultural and political power which the black man must have in order to achieve his survival in a highly developed technical society, and in a world ravaged by imperialism, colonialism, neo-colonialism and fascism.

Black Power epitomises a new stage of revolutionary consciousness of the yearning and aspiration of the black man. Since the black man is the most oppressed of the races of mankind, Black Power, therefore, is the struggle for the possession of the economic, cultural, social and political power which he, in common with the oppressed and the exploited of the earth, must have in order to stampede and overthrow the oppressor. Unless we are prepared to do this then we are prepared to be enslaved.

Your organisation is therefore part of this revolutionary upsurge in the world today.

You are in Britain not by chance or by choice; you are in Britain for historical reasons; you are in Britain because Britain colonised you and reduced the various countries to which you belong to the level of colonial status. You are in Britain because British neo-colonialism is strangling you in your home countries. Where else can you go to seek survival, except in the "mother country" which has enslaved you?

But don't forget that your homes, at the moment, are under the yoke of colonialism or neo-colonialism. You all know that even though your organisations are anti-racist, they face racism in Britain. You have been so long confused that you have become victims of white racism. There is no solution to the race question until all forms of racial discrimination and segregation anywhere are made criminal offences. Under real socialism racism vanishes.

You who are in Britain have a significant role to play in the international black revolutionary movement. You live in the centre of the very citadel of British imperialism and neo-colonialism.

The finger of history is now pointing to the right direction. In my days in London we organised the Coloured Men's Association, and today in the emergence of Black Power you have in Britain organisations like the RASS headed by Michael X and the Black Panther Movement headed by Obi Egbuna. These two organisations are advocates of Black Power, and must mobilise, educate, and re-awaken the black people of Britain to the full realisation of their revolutionary potential.

We know the difficulties you are going through in Britain: discrimination, prejudice and racial hostility. You know that what goes on in Britain, goes on in many parts of the world where white establishment holds power; be it in the United States of America, apartheid South Africa, Latin America, Australia, Rhodesia, Angola, Mozambique, or "Portuguese" Guinea.

Your homes are under puppet regimes teleguided by neo-colonialism. Real black freedom will only come when Africa is politically united. It is only then that the black man will be free to breathe the air of freedom, which is his to breathe, in any part of the world.

To those of you who want to make Britain your home I say, remember that what is important is not where you are but what you do. And to those who want to come back home and fight for Africa's total emancipation, unity and independence I say, come home. We need you.

I want you all to understand that I am not in exile in Conakry. Every country and town in Africa is my home, and so I am at home in Conakry, Guinea, as I would be at home in any part of the black world. I am fit, alive and alert. The struggle for the political unification of Africa has never been clearer and better charted.

You have asked me to be your patron. My answer is, YES. I will stand behind you in all your Black Power revolutionary endeavours, and I hope you will answer my call when the clarion sounds.

I wish you good luck and success.

Africa Day Special Message

AS the armed phase of the African Revolution for total liberation and unity gains momentum in central and southern Africa, racist settlers, imperialists and neo-colonialists are intensifying and diversifying their efforts to consolidate and extend their domination.

They are faced with a protracted guerrilla struggle which in the long run they know they cannot win. But they are seeking by joint military action to contain it, and by devious and insinuating economic and political pentration to undermine its strength.

They see their opportunity in the continuing disunity of independent Africa, the lack of continental planning and direction of the liberation struggle, and in the willingness of certain African leaders to allow their countries to become client states.

Collective imperialism confronts a disunited, weakened, independent Africa.

The situation demands immediate and drastic remedy. We must throw the full weight of a united, revolutionary Africa into the struggle. Each day that we delay, we fail our gallant freedom fighters and betray our people.

It is an open secret that South Africa, Portugal and Rhodesia are co-operating in the military sphere to crush guerrilla campaigns in their territories. They exchange information about freedom fighter activities, allow overflights and landings of military aircraft in each other's countries, and in the case of South Africa, supply armed forces and helicopters to assist in the counter-offensive.

A military intelligence board, known as the Council of Three, is said to meet regularly in Pretoria, Salisbury, Lourenco Marques or Luanda, to prepare joint action.

The world first heard of the participation of South African forces in military action outside their own borders in August 1967, when a strong force of freedom fighters went into action around the Wankie game reserve in Rhodesia. A large contingent of South African police in armoured cars was rushed to the scene.

Since then, there have been innumerable reports of South African intervention. In Rhodesia, South West Africa, Angola and Mozambique, South African helicopters are being used to hunt freedom fighters. Armed South African police are operating against nationalists in South West Africa. South African troops are reported in both Angola and Mozambique.

Nor is enemy co-operation confined to defensive operations. There are clear indications that the members of the Council of Three are planning offensive action against independent states.

Zambia has been openly threatened. Furthermore, some ten miles from her border, on the Caprivi strip, the South Africans have built an enormous airfield, said to have a two mile runway. There are many reports of armed incursions of Rhodesians, South Africans and Portuguese over the borders between Zambia, Rhodesia and Mozambique.

The example of the recent Israeli aggression against Arab states has not passed unnoticed in Pretoria, and has been publicly proclaimed in South Africa as an effective way of dealing with a so-called "threat" from neighbouring states.

Faced with the combined military strength of the South Africans, Portuguese and Rhodesian settlers, African freedom fighters must close their ranks and put an end to internecine rivalries. They must also be supported by united and determined action on the part of the whole of independent Africa.

No part of Africa is free while any of our national territory remains unliberated. There can be no co-existence between African independence and imperialist and neo-colonialist domination; between independent Africa and racist, minority, settler governments.

The military obstacles we have to overcome if we are to achieve our goal of total liberation and an All-African Union Government are obvious and surmountable. Less easy to recognise and to combat are the insidious, often disguised workings of neo-colonialism—the economic and political pressures which seek to undermine our independence and to perpetuate and extend the grip of foreign monopoly finance capital over the economic life of our continent.

Many of our so-called independent states are in fact neo-colonies. They have all the outward appearance of sovereignty, but their economy and therefore their political policy is directed from outside.

Some have been in the grip of neo-colonialism since independence. Others have been subjected to neo-colonialism by means of military coups engineered by neo-colonialists acting in conjunction with indigenous reactionaries.

In recent months, with the intensification of the guerrilla struggle in central and southern Africa, pressure has been strongly directed towards those states which have common frontiers with South Africa, Rhodesia, Angola and Mozambique. The object is to dominate them politically and economically, and thus hold up the advance of the African Revolution and at the same time to improve their own neo-colonialist position.

The tragedy is that some African heads of state are themselves actually aiding and abetting imperialists and neo-colonialists. In February 1967 Malawi became the first independent African state to conclude a trade agreement, and later to establish diplomatic relations with South Africa.

Since then, other African states have also been lured into the South African neo-colonialist web by a mixture of "aid" and carefully-veiled threats.

The withdrawal of Britain from the High Commission territories, the break between Britain and Rhodesia as a result of UDI, and the outbreak of guerrilla warfare in the Portuguese colonies, has given South Africa a golden opportunity to jump in.

South Africa is in the classic, imperialist position of a manufacturing country seeking new outlets for its capital and goods. Its policy is to exploit the labour and resources of its hinterland, thereby strengthening South Africa's economy and at the same time delaying the advance of the African Revolution.

South Africa's "new policy" of improved relations with African states has been described as the building of "bridges" rather than "forts". The crux of the matter was revealed clearly in the editorial of the South African "Financial Gazette" of May 10, 1968:

"We must build more bridges and less forts. The might of our armed forces are not enough to shield off hostilities still being built up against South Africa in some African states. We must build more bridges into Africa. In Malawi we have virtually spanned a bridge into the heart of Africa".

A delighted broadcaster in Salisbury on October 8, 1967 praised Dr. Banda for what he called his "realistic policy", and added: "the nations which are nearest to South Africa have been the quickest to realise the side on which their bread is buttered". He referred here to Lesotho and Botswana.

South Africa is daily increasing her economic and political penetration into African territories. The Lesotho government in 1967 appointed three South Africans to "advise" on political and economic affairs. In Rhodesia, South African capital investment already exceeds that of Britain; and it is mainly the support of South Africa which has enabled Ian Smith's rebel regime to survive.

The South African government has recently granted eight million rand to Malawi for the building of the new capital city at Lilongwe. Of the five million rand set aside for "economic co-operation" two million has already been ear-marked for Malawi as a "first instalment" this year.

Since 1964, when Malawi became independent, imports from South Africa have doubled; while the main force behind capital investment in Malawi is increasingly the South African government itself.

The South African liberation movement together with the peoples of independent Africa and freedom fighters wherever they are operating must be alert to this new challenge. Neo-colonialism, like colonialism and imperialism can only be banished from our midst by armed struggle.

In east, central and west Africa, neo-colonialism is hard at work fostering regional economic groupings, in the knowledge that without political cohesion they will remain weak and subject to neo-colonialist pressures and domination. The U.S. government in its latest statement on "aid" has said that it will favour those states which are grouped together in this way.

As each new attempt is made to divide us and to divert us from our purpose, it must be exposed and attacked. Already, the ordinary men and women of Africa are talking the language of the African Revolution. They speak of freedom, unity and socialism, and know that these objectives are synonymous, and can only be attained through armed struggle.

In some cases, the people of Africa are ahead of their governments. But the pressures they are exerting will inevitably compel the pace forward.

We must recognise and fight the external and the internal enemy, and combine all our resources in the great struggle which lies ahead. With cohesive planning and with a full awareness of our united strength, nothing can halt the progress towards final victory.

Ghana: The Way Out

PEOPLE of Ghana, the NLC must be forcibly overthrown now, by Positive Action in the form of a counter-coup if our beloved country is to be saved from complete political, social and economic disintegration. The time for non-violent action has passed. A quick, knock-out blow must now be delivered to clear the way for a radical, new, national reconstruction.

In this immense task of reconstruction we shall need the active participation of every single Ghanaian who has the will to work, and the love of country to wish to make Ghana great and prosperous. No one need fear revenge and time-wasting recrimination. The slate has been wiped clean. We must start afresh in the light of the tragic experience of the past two years. New thinking and action is needed.

As each day passes, Ghana is being dragged further and further down into the mud. The independent economy we strove so hard to build has broken down completely.

There is large-scale unemployment. All indigenous development has stopped, and the puppet NLC has handed over our national assets one by one to foreign interests. Almost a hundred state corporations have been sold.

You have seen with your own eyes the shameful disposal of Ghana's assets. Our state hotels are now foreign owned. The 20-mile rubber plantation developed by the State Farms Corporation has been handed over to the Firestone Rubber Company of America. The whole economic situation is the negation of an independent economic policy, and a downright sell-out to American and other foreign, capitalist financial interests.

The balance of payments problem is being tackled in the classic capitalist way of creating unemployment and devaluation of the cedi. Unemployment suits capitalism.

It is an excellent thing for so-called private enterprise. It weakens the bargaining power of the workers (who have only their labour to sell), and it makes sure of a steady pool of cheap labour.

The basic principle of capitalism and so-called private enterprise (which in Africa generally means foreign private enterprise) is that an industrial or commercial project shall depend for its initiation or continuance according to how much profit it makes for the individual or group of individuals, such as shareholders. Capitalists or private entrepreneurs always seek projects which provide them with the greatest profit for the least investment in the shortest time. This is the principle on which they operate.

It means that in Ghana they are only going to support or introduce such projects as will show them the maximum possible profits for the smallest effort in the shortest time, and in the most convenient place to fulfil these conditions.

They are not going to do something in Ghana if they can do it more cheaply and with greater profit somewhere else. Nor are they going to do it in Ghana if it is in competition with some similar project they already have somewhere else.

This is why the treacherous NLC has failed completely in persuading its foreign capitalist sponsors to undertake a single new project in Ghana. All they have succeeded in doing is to allow foreign capitalists to take over certain existing projects which were already extremely profitable, or which were already at such a stage of development that they are certain to show a good profit in the near future.

This is why the incompetent NLC has had to close down or seriously curtail a whole series of our national projects which are of no interest to foreign profiteers. And why it has had to cut down social services, including education and health, to a point where they are in danger of total collapse. It has even become necessary now to pay a visiting fee when calling to see relatives and friends in hospital.

What foreign capitalists like about the ignorant NLC is that they have provided them with free access to Ghana's raw materials, and a plentiful supply of cheap labour to pick and choose as they wish. These are the classical conditions of colonialism. They are also the conditions of neo-colonialism, which is only the old colonialism with a facade of African stooges.

National development is impossible under this system. How can we develop Ghana as a whole if the test of every project is its attractiveness to foreign investors and its rapid profitability? Which foreign investor is going to develop the Northern Region of Ghana, for example, when the quickest source of profit is in the Southern Region?

The terrible neglect which is now taking place in large areas in Ghana is a direct result of neo-colonialist policies, and the abandonment of the principles of socialist planning. Even around Accra, which is economically convenient to capitalists, nothing of real value is taking place because foreign capitalists do not find it profitable enough. All they have done so far is to take over the industries and state enterprises which we worked so hard to build.

Ghana is no longer being run by an African government; it is being administered by a small clique of corrupt army and police officers, and behind the Ghanaian facade, the decisions are being made by foreign interests. There are some 250 American "experts" in Ghana who are actively aiding and advising the NLC. The U.S. Ambassador in Accra attends all official functions, and occupies a position similar to that held by the French official advisers in the Francophone states.

During last year, it is estimated that the U.S. government and the I.M.F. provided 70 million dollars credit to bolster up the regime. A team of economists from Harvard has had the effrontery to advise a "development" plan for Ghana. What a miserable substitute for our own Seven Year Development Plan, drawn up by economists dedicated solely to the interests and welfare of the Ghanaian people.

Our economic problems are not being treated as Ghanaian problems, but as the problems of the United States of America, Britain, West Germany and other countries which have substantial economic interests in Ghana.

The solutions being dictated by advisers from these countries are not intended to strengthen the economy in the interests of the people of Ghana, but in the interests of the foreign companies and governments which today dominate and exploit the treachery and ignorance of the NLC. Ghana has become a neo-colony.

Mass unemployment has led to a crime wave of a type previously unknown in the history of our country. With growing unemployment and rising prices, living conditions have become intolerable. Many Ghanaians are finding it impossible to earn a living or to get enough food to eat. Groups of desperate men, some of them armed, are roaming the countryside at will, and in many places our peaceful citizens cannot travel in safety, or even sleep securely in their beds at night. Thus, formerly peaceful citizens have become criminals in order to survive.

The democratic pretences of the NLC are exposed by the deceptive draft constitution which they have produced after two years of misrule. This is a further attempt to deceive the Ghanaian people and to pull the wool over their eyes. It solves nothing. Under the infamous Disenfranchisement Decree thousands of Ghanaians are to be denied the vote and banned from the political life of the country simply because they are members of the Convention People's Party and believe in socialism. Hiding behind the cloak of a so-called civilian government there will remain the same clique of traitors and their neo-colonialist manipulators.

Yet the implementation of even these phoney constitutional proposals have been put off into the indefinite future, the NLC admitting that a return to civilian rule could "hardly bear realistic examination". The truth is that the traitorous clique dare not permit any form of popular political activity, even though the CPP and all its wing organisations have been banned.

The NLC and their foreign masters know how tenuous is the authority they wield, and fear that any genuinely free political expression would immediately bring about their total collapse.

Under my government, all our policies were devised and implemented with one object only, to promote the well-being and happiness of the Ghanaian people as a whole, and to strive to bring about the complete liberation of Africa and the establishment of an All-African Union Government.

The result of that method of thinking and planning is apparent to you all. You have only to look around you to see what we achieved. We built more roads, bridges and other forms of national communication than any other independent African state. We built more schools, clinics and hospitals. We provided more clean, piped water. We trained more teachers, doctors and nurses. We established more industries.

In the first nine years of independence our country was transformed. From a colony subsisting mainly on agriculture, notably cocoa-growing, it had become a dynamic independent state with a diversified and rapidly expanding economy.

Hundreds of thousands of acres of more land were brought into cultivation. With state and co-operative farming, with modern technology and irrigation schemes, agriculture was boosted and food production increased.

We launched the Workers Brigade, a national service organisation whereby young men and women and workers without employment could play a decisive part in Ghana's national construction. With the plans for industrialisation, there was need to train artisans and builders in public construction work to supplement Ghana's manpower. Feeder roads and dams were built, and farms were under cultivation by the Workers Brigade.

Education was free at all levels and students in teacher training colleges and universities received additional monthly allowances to meet their private expenses. Three universities were established, and the student population rose to 5,000. Plans were nearing completion for the building of a University of Agriculture at Somanya.

According to a UNESCO Report in 1963, Ghana spent more on education in proportion to her size and population than any country in the world.

Medical facilities were, to a large extent, free; and the many hospitals, clinics, child welfare centres and nurseries are there for all to see.

As you know, one of my main preoccupations was the electrification of Ghana—for without abundant electric power large-scale industrialisation such as we envisaged was impossible. Always in the forefront of my mind, therefore, was the vital importance of the Volta River Project. Completion of this mighty multi-purpose project was the key to all our dreams of an economically independent Ghana.

It was no mere coincidence that it was only a few weeks after the completion of the Volta River Project in its initial stage of providing hydroelectric power, that traitors and neo-colonialists struck to destroy everything for which we had worked so long.

Plans were far advanced for the construction of the Bui dam, and for other smaller dams in various parts of the country. Ghana was at the point of breakthrough into national economic self-reliance.

Our national assets had never stood so high. We had laid the infrastructure for the development of Ghana into a modern, industrial state. Our real wealth—our roads, communications, Tema harbour, the Volta River Project, our educational and public health systems, our factories, state corporations, hotels and public buildings—was reflected in actual achievement and in productive potential.

Economic experts the world over, unless the tools of vested commercial interests, acknowledged that the progress we had made in Ghana was amazing and beyond what even the most optimistic had believed possible.

But for the treachery of the NLC, the whole of Ghana would by now have been electrified. Industrialisation would have taken place not only in the South, but in every region including the far North. Every town and village would have had ample electricity and piped water. There would have been further expansion of both the health and education services.

There would have been a tremendous increase in food production. We had development plans for the vast grasslands of the North. Only days before the "coup", I had signed a contract for the irrigation and agricutural development of the Accra plains. Our scheme to create an inland fishing industry and inland water transport on the Volta Lake was near to operation. We were waiting only for the water to rise.

All these schemes, and they were nation-wide, would have required the active participation of tens of thousands more of our people. Every young man and woman was needed as soon as he or she had completed the necessary education. How criminal that our resources of people and materials should now be wasted in mass unemployment, and that our immense productive potential should be put at the disposal of neo-colonialists serving their own selfish interests.

The Ghanaian, who was before a proud African, courageous and with head held high, today appears head-bowed as a collaborator with neo-colonialists. He is suffering as a result of the shame that has been brought on Ghana by the imperialist-inspired coup of February 24, 1966.

Ghana, under my government, was a haven for the oppressed from all parts of Africa. Freedom fighters trained there. Ghana was revered all over the African continent, as a country which all who fought oppression and exploitation could depend upon. Our political and economic achievements were closely studied and admired.

Today, Ghana might not exist for all the impact the country makes in Africa and in world affairs. It is as if the heart has been torn out of the body, and only a lifeless robot remains, the mechanism controlled by a clique of traitors who in their turn are slavishly following the instructions of their neo-colonialist masters.

Yet there is no need to despair or to abandon hope. We have the mind, the will and the means to rebuild our country for the prosperity and happiness of all our people. All that stands in the way is the NLC and their abject subservience to foreign exploiters.

People of Ghana, stir yourselves. Rise up as free men and women. Be proud of your heritage and of your national independence. What the criminal NLC has destroyed can be rebuilt. Our development plans can once again be put into operation.

I have been following events in Ghana very closely. The economic situation is very serious, but it is not beyond recovery if action is taken quickly. Recently, Sierra Leone has shown the world how a corrupt military-police dictatorship can be removed, and constitutional government restored. Those who carried out the removal of the military junta in Sierra Leone were not even high-ranking officers. They were from the lower ranks of the army.

But they possessed the necessary ingredient for complete victory: true patriotism and the confidence of knowing that they were fulfilling the wishes of the vast majority of the people.

I have not been wasting my time in Conakry. I have been working studying and drawing up plans for the reconstruction of our country. I am able to tell you, as a result of my very deep study of the economic situation, that it would be possible to put Ghana on the road again towards meaningful economic progress in a matter not of years, but of a few months.

You will not expect me to tell you in any sort of detail of the plan I have worked out. To do so would open the door for foreign vested interests to prepare new sabotage. Your own common sense will tell you that things have gone basically wrong in Ghana, and that a completely new approach is needed.

I would like everybody to organise in secret groups. Organise in the villages and in the localities in the towns. Organise at your work places. Organise in your trade unions. The power of the people is irresistible once it is organised. Nothing can withstand it. The majority of the army and police are behind me and long for my early return to Ghana. Tribalism should not be allowed to confuse the issue.

The NLC must be overthrown now. There is no other way, than by force, to liberate our country from neo-colonialism and its stooges. Only then can the great work of national reconstruction again begin, and Ghana once more assume its true role in Africa and in world affairs.

Long live Ghana, and long live Africa's total emancipation and unity!

"Civilian Rule" Fraud

THE so-called NLC has it back to the wall. Therefore, in a last desperate attempt to save itself the Liars' Council announced, on May 22 its programme for the country's return to civilian rule by September 30, 1969.

Let no one be deceived for one moment by this bogus and dishonest gesture. The last thing the NLC and their neo-colonialist masters intend is to allow genuinely free and democratic elections. This would be equivalent to agreeing to their own extinction, because they know that Ghanaians would vote overwhelmingly for an end to the shameful exploitation of Ghana, and for a restoration of constitutional government.

What the NLC hopes to achieve by this latest attempt to deceive the people of Ghana is time—time in which to try to prop up their own tottering edifice; to complete the final sell-out of the rights and aspirations of the people of Ghana to foreign interests; and to fabricate some facade of civilian rule behind which the same traitors and neo-colonialists can continue to operate.

The Liars' Council must be allowed no more time. Already they have had over two years in whch to follow their selfish, corrupt and destructive pursuits. During this time, Ghana's assets have been sold to foreign interests, and the independent economy we were working so hard to build is in danger of being irrevocably destroyed. Ghana, once in the vanguard of the African Revolution, is now of no account, a neo-colony run by a clique of army and police traitors.

The time has come to act. Ghana must be saved, and saved NOW by a quick, decisive blow in the form of a counter-coup. This is the urgent responsibility of the officers and rank-and-file of the army and police who are still loyal to the cause of Ghana. The Trade Unions and workers of Ghana must also play their part by organising a nation-wide general strike.

Examination of the NLC's so-called "programme" for the return to civilian rule reveals the sham civilian government they have in mind. For example, elections for the Constituent Assembly, the body to be responsible for finalising the new constitution for Ghana, are to be on a non-party basis.

In other words, there is to be no lifting of the ban on political activity until AFTER the Constituent Assembly has completed its work and the new constitution has been promulgated and imposed by the NLC on the people of Ghana.

Ghanaians are, therefore, to have a constitution approved by a Constituent Assembly which can, under no stretch of the imagination, be said to represent them. What an insult, that Ghanaians should be treated with such contempt and deprived of the fundamental right of a people to have a constitution of their own choosing.

In denying the right of Ghanaians to hold popular elections for the establishing of the Constituent Assembly, the NLC is not even carrying out the recommendations of its own Constitutional Commission. This Commission recommended that the Constituent Assembly should be established "by popular elections", and that it "should be the people's representative body in a truly democratic sense".

No details have been given in the May 22 announcement as to how the Constituent Assembly is to be formed, but it is obvious that elections cannot be either "popular" or "democratic" if all political activity is banned.

It is only after the non-representative Constituent Assembly has concluded its work that Ghanaians are to be allowed to prepare for elections to the National Assembly. Here again, the wording of the NLC statement is intentionally vague and full of loopholes. The success of the elections to the National Assembly will depend, so the NLC says, "mainly on the speed and thoroughness with which the electoral commissioner carries out his assignment".

Fresh electoral registers will have to be drawn up, and this "should take about four months". The NLC "hopes" that the Constituent Assembly will be able to conclude its work within three months, thus "making it possible for a civilian government to be installed not later than September 30, 1969".

Meantime all political activity is banned for more than another year, and there is no guarantee that the ban will be lifted then.

Those who have studied the draft constitutional proposals drawn up by the NLC Constitutional Commission know the fraudulent constitution the NLC proposes to place before the Constituent Assembly. Note the all-powerful Judiciary, and the powers of the "President" who will have under his "control" and "supervision" certain departments and organs of government which will be virtually independent of the government of the day.

Note the powers of the Council of State, appointed, not elected, which is to be a body of so-called "prominent citizens" advising the "President". And note also, the provision made for the inclusion in the Cabinet of ministers from outside the National Assembly, i.e. ministers with no shred of a mandate from the electorate.

To add insult to injury, an Elections and Public Offices Disqualification Decree has been issued by which thousands of Ghanaians are to be banned for ten years from holding public office simply because they were members of the CPP and believe in socialism. The ban extends not only to all former CPP office holders, but to members of the Party's integral wings —the United Farmers Co-operative Council, the Trade Union Congress, the National Union of Ghana Women, the Ghana Young Pioneers Movement, the National Association of Socialist Students Organisation, the League of Ghana Patriots, and the Young Farmers League.

Exemption from the Disqualification Decree, we are told, can only be obtained if the Exemptions Commissions is satisfied the person was either forced into membership of the CPP, or can show that he was actively opposing the Party while a member of it!

This then is the kind of "civilian government" the NLC has in mind. Hiding behind the cloak of so-called "civilian government" there will remain the same traitors and their neo-colonialist and imperialist masters.

But even these latest phoney constitutional proposals are unlikely to be implemented in the time stated. The time limit of May and September 1969 is mere fantasy, just as the two years limit set by this same Notorious Liars Council in February 1966 has turned out to be a mere pipe dream.

Military regimes the world over make a habit of proclaiming their intentions to return to civilian rule and to hold elections, but in not a single case has this been done. By their very nature, these regimes are incapable of organising a genuine return to constitutional government. Having seized power by force they are never likely to hand over to a civilian government through a freely conducted general election. In the face of such a government they would stand condemned.

They may talk of "free elections" but this is simply to deceive the masses and to discourage resistance. As has already happened, any election result considered to be "unfavourable" to an army and police regime is instantly declared null and void.

In Dahomey, a return to civilian rule was promised by June 17, 1968. But this time limit has been abandoned in view of the fiasco of the presidential elections held on May 5, when all previous office-holders, including the three leaders of the former political parties were excluded and only 24 per cent of the electorate voted.

In Togo where a return to civilian rule has also been discussed, President Eyadema has made it clear that he intends to continue to maintain army rule.

In Upper Volta, the army has declared its intention of continuing in power until 1970.

Sierra Leone is at present the only country which has successfully returned to civilian rule, and it is significant that this was achieved NOT as the result of elections but by means of an army counter-coup. Swift action by a group of non-commissioned officers overthrew the military-police dictatorship and invited Mr. Siaka Stevens, the winner of the 1967 general election in Sierra Leone to form a government.

In a single night the people of Sierra Leone were rid of the clique of army and police traitors who had betrayed them. This example of Sierra Leone should inspire and encourage comparable action in other states suffering under similar conditions.

In Ghana, the NLC has by its announcement of May 22 had the impudence to call on the people to show their "political maturity" in a "peaceful and orderly transition" to civilian rule. Thus, cynically and contemptuously, they have addressed themselves to the same people they condemned and abused a year ago as being "ignorant of their rights".

This being so, the people of Ghana must show their political maturity and their awareness of their rights by taking the only effective and logical course open to them: the forcible overthrow of the NLC by a counter-coup.

This is the only way to save Ghana NOW. The masses are awakened and are ready waiting to hail the downfall of their betrayers, and to begin the great task of national reconstruction.

Long live Ghana.

There is victory for us.

A Call For Positive Action and Armed Struggle

COMRADES and militants of the Convention People's Party. Greetings.

The beginning of 1966 found Ghana poised for a break-through in her national economy. As Ghana's economic progress gained momentum so did the imperialist neo-colonialist intrigues and subversion increase. Our experienced Party, however, was equal to the tasks and the challenges. Ghana became an inspiring spearhead of the African revolution.

The situation of Ghana since February 24, 1966 has been a chronicle of mass unemployment, sadness, shame, incompetence and chaos. Proud Ghanaians now walk about with heads bowed down in shame.

Ghana is sold out and is in the grip of neo-colonialists and their lackeys. Everything is in continuing collapse and tribalism has raised its head again.

The breakdown is further aggravated by a selfish struggle for power by individuals of political mediocrity and discredited politicians. And now the neo-colonialist noose is strangling Ghana!

The puppet "NLC" stand aghast and trembling at bay. They have bitten off too much and face catastrophe. And so they cling fast to their neo-colonialist advisers whose advice leads them on to more and more chaos and disillusionment.

For us, the militant of the Party, to sit down doing nothing and watch twenty years hard work with concrete achievements destroyed by a short-sighted and corrupt few, is infamy and downright cowardice.

Ghana must be saved. The return to power of the Party and its popular government is the only way to save Ghana now. And this cannot be done constitutionally.

I have closely and carefully followed the collapsing trends in Ghana. I have deliberately kept silent all this time because I know the time has not yet come for me say anything. We shall soon have a great deal to say—very soon.

Our militants are everywhere in Ghana. The time for words is past. Now is the time for action. Comrades, you have a mission to perform.

I enjoin you to stand firm and prepare for the final struggle. Organise now. United we can destroy the NLC. Form your secret cells in your localities, in your work-places, wherever you are. Prepare for the day of liberation.

Remember that the majority of the army and police are behind us.

Against the united power of the masses, the NLC is powerless. But you must organise in readiness. Prepare to organise strikes, demonstrations, seizure of key public buildings and other places in support of armed action.

Prepare now. You will know when to act.

This is a time for Positive Action inside Ghana: Positve Action by the workers—by the awakened masses. By Positive Action we were able to overthrow British colonialism in Ghana and by Positive Action we can dislodge the blind and short-sighted neo-colonialist puppet regime now in Ghana.

One thing we comp'etely reject is any idea of a so-called general election. No one is taken in by the vague and foxy promises of "a return to civilian rule". Nobody is deceived by any new "constitution".

The neo-colonialist intentions of the "NLC" are proven by their so-called "disqualification decree". If they believe in free elections and are not afraid of the power of the CPP, why have they banned and disfranchised the CPP?

Constitutions are powerless before guns. Prior to February 24, 1966, who would have thought that a few misdirected soldiers of our Ghana Armed Forces could overthrow the legally constituted government of Ghana and destroy overnight twenty years work of concrete achievements?

We have passed from constitutional non-violent Positive Action to Positive Action by force and armed struggle.

Indeed, it would be utter madness to even consider general elections under military dictatorship. "Coup" makers must be repaid in kind. The only real and permanent way to save Ghana is by the forcible overthrow of the "NLC". This is the only way by which we can save Ghana from the madness of neo-colonialism and its lackeys. All other ways are blind alleys.

Down with imperialism and neo-colonialism!
Long live the awakened masses of Ghana!
Long live our revolutionary Party!
THERE IS VICTORY FOR US! !

To
Ernesto Ché Guevara
Ben Barka
Malcolm X

We could mourn them
 but they don't want our tears.
We scorn death knowing
 that we cannot be defeated.

Introduction

PAN-AFRICANISM has its beginnings in the liberation struggle of African-Americans, expressing the aspirations of Africans and peoples of African descent. From the first Pan-African Conference, held in London in 1900, until the fifth and last Pan-African Conference held in Manchester in 1945, African-Americans provided the main driving power of the movement. Pan-Africanism then moved to Africa, its true home, with the holding of the First Conference of Independent African States in Accra in April 1958, and the All-African Peoples' Conference in December of the same year.

The work of the early pioneers of Pan-Africanism such as H. Sylvester Williams, Dr. W. E. B. Du Bois, Marcus Garvey, and George Padmore, none of whom were born in Africa, has become a treasured part of Africa's history. It is significant that two of them, Dr. Du Bois and George Padmore, came to live in Ghana at my invitation. Dr. Du Bois died, as he wished, on African soil, while working in Accra on the Encyclopedia Africana. George Padmore became my Adviser on African Affairs, and spent the last years of his life in Ghana, helping in the revolutionary struggle for African unity and socialism.

The close links forged between Africans and peoples of African descent over half a century of common struggle continue to inspire and strengthen us. For, although the outward forms of our struggle may change, it remains in essence the same, a fight to the death against oppression, racism and exploitation.

Most of Africa has now achieved political independence. But imperialism has not been vanquished. International finance capital appearing now in its new guise of neo-colonialism seeks to maintain and extend its stranglehold over the economic life of our continent. Imperialists and neo-colonialists are resorting to every kind of stratagem to achieve their purposes. They have allied with reactionary elements in our midst to organise military coups and other forms of direct action in an attempt to halt the progress of the African Revolution. They are at the same time working in more insidious ways to undermine our morale and to divert our attention from the main purpose of our struggle—the total liberation of the African continent, an All-African Union Government and socialism.

The Organisation of African Unity has been rendered virtually useless as a result of the machinations of neo-colonialists and their puppets. Yet it is being preserved as an innocuous organisation in the hope that it may delay the formation of a really effective Pan-African organisation which will lead to genuine political unification. Encouragement is being given to the formation of African regional economic organisations in the knowledge that without political cohesion they will be ineffective and serve to strengthen, not weaken, neo-colonialist exploitation and domination.

All manner of red herrings are being used to distract and deflect us from our purpose. There is talk of "African socialism", Arab socialism, democratic socialism, Muslim socialism, and latterly, the "pragmatic pattern of development", their advocates claiming they have found the solution to our problems.

Just as there is only one true socialism, scientific socialism, the principles of which are universal and abiding, there is only one way to achieve the African revolutionary goals of liberation, political unification and socialism. That way lies through armed struggle. The time for speechifying, for conferences, for makeshift solutions and for compromise is past.

Similarly, with the emergence of Black Power in the United States of America, the liberation movement of African-Americans has become militant and armed. But as in Africa, the movement is having to be on its guard against the internal as well as the external enemy. There must be a closing of ranks and tenacious, united effort to carry the struggle through to a successful conclusion.

The Spectre of Black Power

WITH a decisiveness and force which can no longer be concealed the spectre of Black Power has descended on the world like a thundercloud flashing its lightning. Emerging from the ghettoes, swamps and cotton-fields of America, it now haunts the streets, legislative assemblies and high councils and has so shocked and horrified Americans that it is only now that they are beginning to grasp its full significance, and the fact that Black Power, in other manifestations, is in confrontation with imperialism, colonialism, neo-colonialism, exploitation and aggression in many parts of the world.

In America, the "Negro problem" has been a more or less polite conversation piece since the first African slaves were landed in James Town in 1619. For three hundred and fifty years, however, the subject of "slave revolts" has been tabooed and eliminated from text-books. For the past thirty years stringent efforts have been made to whitewash and obscure the real issue of the United States Civil War: whether African slavery should be continued or not. Indeed, it is no longer considered proper in the United States to mention the "Civil War". Polite references are sometimes made to the "unfortunate war between the states".

After the Civil War, the 13th, 14th and 15th Amendments to the United States Constitution did abolish African slavery and granted citizenship rights to the freed men. Immediately, the majority of states passed laws nullifying these rights, and in general, public opinion all over the country supported their action. There were some legislators who pointed out the injustice and even dangers of this course, and in 1875 Congress passed a mild Civil Rights Bill for the freed men. But in 1884 this Bill was repealed by the United States Supreme Court. And so, down through the years, people of African descent in the United States of America have been petitioning, pleading, going to court and demonstrating for "rights" freely granted to every naturalised immigrant.

As the United States grew richer, more powerful and imperialistic, as it expanded and extended its influence and control throughout Latin America and the islands of the Caribbean, its racialism, oppression and contempt for the peoples of African descent became accepted as an American way of life.

Russia's October Revolution did not penetrate the masses of African-Americans. A few intellectuals, however, did hail it as a triumph of the oppressed and the exploited, a proletarian socialist victory. Some travelled to the newly established Soviet Union. Several remained there, and contributed their strengh and skills in building the world's first socialist state. But those who returned found no means of applying what they had seen to the situation in the United States. Meanwhile, white workers were agitating for better working conditions. But until the organisation of the Committee for Industrial Organisation (C.I.O.) and the Second World War, African-Americans were regularly excluded from labour organisations. The need for increased manpower during this period encouraged immigration from the South of thousands of black workers who crowded into northern cities finding jobs, but no place to live except in slums amid conditions far worse than the rural shacks they had left in the South.

In spite of the long and untiring work in education and organisation of the pioneers of "Civil Rights"; in spite of the painstaking efforts made by African-American citizens of the United States to educate their children,

Smoke rises above the Negro ghetto of Watts in the city of Los Angeles when "African-Americans took up arms to meet their aggressors".

and by hard work to achieve "acceptance" in American society, African-Americans have remained only barely tolerated aliens in the land of their birth, the vast mass of them outside consideration of basic human justice.

This is a fact which is now being called to the attention of all those who through the years have had in their power the means to order and fashion the world according to their interests. White interests controlled the economic wealth; white interests have been able to establish the "moral" standards by which America must live; white domestic imperialism made all the laws, rules and regulations. This was the modern world up to, and throughout, the first half of the twentieth century.

The independence of Ghana, achieved on March 6, 1957, ushered in the decisive struggle for freedom and independence throughout Africa—

Another scene in Watts during the fighting which took place in August 1965.

freedom from colonial rule and settler domination. On that day I proclaimed to the world "the independence of Ghana is meaningless unless it is linked with the total liberation of the African continent." Immediately, the beating drums sent this message across rivers, mountains, forests and plains. The people heard and acted. Liberation movements gained strength, and freedom fighters began to train. One after another, new African states came into being, and above the world's horizon loomed the African Personality. African statesmen went to the United Nations; Africans proudly wore the ancient regalia of their ancestral land; Africans stood up and spoke on the rostrum of the world forum, and they spoke for Africans and the people of African descent wherever they might be.

I experienced the immediate impact on Africa's dispossessed in the United States—Black dignity could be achieved. Black beauty was a reality. I know how determined and inspired African-American students went out from their colleges in the South and "sat down" in those places which laws and customs had reserved for "whites" only. They were heard to say when they were being dragged to jail by infuriated police: "All Africa will be liberated before we here can get a lousy cup of coffee!"

American text-books shy away from discussion of slave revolts, though riots and insurrection form a large part of African-American history. We know how black men and women fought through the swamps of Louisiana, how Virginian planters cowed before the name of the rebel, Nat Turner, how Harriet Tubman led armed bands of runaway slaves out of the South, and of her fame as a sharp-shooter. The largest slave revolt was planned and led by a white man whose name has been immortalised in song. It was on Harpers Ferry bridge that John Brown began the Civil War which led inevitably to the freeing of the slaves.

The young African-American "sit-downers" of recent years committed no violence, nor did the many white students who, following their example, poured out of the great northern universities to demonstrate against racialism, segregation and discrimination. But their petitions and pleas for justice were met with violence, with savage beatings, with jail sentences. Some of them died in the struggle.

Then, on August 18, 1965, in the Negro ghetto of Watts, in the city of Los Angeles, African-Americans took up arms to meet their aggressors. Since then, practically every major city in the United States has seen guns, rifles and fire bombs in the hands of black men, who, with every shot fired, are claiming their birthright. Since 1966, the cry of the rebellion has been "Black Power".

What is Black Power? I see it in the United States as part of the vanguard of world revolution against capitalism, imperialism and neo-colonialism which have enslaved, exploited and oppressed peoples everywhere, and against which the masses of the world are now revolting. Black Power is part of the world rebellion of the oppressed against the oppressor, of the exploited against the exploiter. It operates throughout the African continent, in North and South America, the Caribbean, wherever Africans and people of African descent live. It is linked with the Pan-African struggle for unity on the African continent, and with all those who strive to establish a socialist society.

Analysis of the United States social structure indicates that black Americans comprise the proletariat base of the country. On their backs, their toil, sweat, enslavement and exploitation have been built the wealth, prosperity and high standard of living enjoyed by America today. Until recently, African-Americans sought to alleviate their oppression through

The late Malcolm X. He was shot and killed while addressing a meeting in New York.

integration into the majority white population. They demonstrated for an end of social discrimination and for "equal rights", wanting to gain access to schools and colleges, restaurants, hotels and other places from which they had been excluded. Such were the demands of the Civil Rights Movement. Yet large numbers of African-Americans had no jobs, no decent housing, and no money to enjoy the restaurants, hotels and swimming pools reserved for "whites only". The Civil Rights Movement did not speak for the needs of the African-American masses.

It was, however, thought that the plea for civil rights would be met, because the United States Constitution, with its various amendments, supports these demands. Instead, thousands of African-Americans have been jailed, intimidated, beaten, and some murdered for agitating for those rights guaranteed by the American constitution.

The masses grasp instinctively the meaning and goal of Black Power: the oppressed and exploited are *without power*. Those who have power have everything, those without power have nothing: if you don't believe in guns, you are already dead.

Black Power gives the African-American an entirely new dimension. It is a vanguard movement of black people, but it opens the way for all oppressed masses. Unfortunately, the Trade Unions in the United States are as capitalist in make-up and goals as any million dollar corporation. And the majority of white skilled workers with their well-furnished houses, two cars, televisions and long vacations are complacent. They have much more to "lose than their chains". But there are potentially revolutionary white masses in the United States. Consider the lot of the "poor whites" in the hills of Georgia, Tennessee and the Carolinas, the white sharecroppers in the lowlands of Alabama and Mississippi. Too often these are written off as "poor white trash". But they, too, are dispossessed; often they are without hope. Yet "poor whites" and "blacks" have not been pushed as far down as their backs will lie. When they see a way ahead for them, the oppressed and exploited do revolt. Black Power is leading the way; Black Power is already a spearhead.

At this momentous period of history, as the era of peoples armed revolution gets under way in Africa, I see coming the triumph of the human spirit, the collapse of the forces of inhumanity and the emergence of the glorious effort finally to free mankind from senseless and inhuman exploitation, degradation and wars. The old Africa is crumbling down; the new Africa is being constructed.

In Africa, we thought we could achieve freedom and independence, and our ultimate goals of unity and socialism by peaceful means. This has landed us in the grip of neo-colonialism. We could not succeed using non-violent methods. The same power structure which is blocking the efforts of African-Americans in the United States is also now throwing road-blocks in Africa's way. Imperialism, neo-colonialism, settler domination and racialism seek to bring us down and re-subjugate us.

In Africa, Latin America, the Caribbean, the Middle East and South East Asia, imperialists and neo-colonialists, with the help of local stooges, attempt to master with guns. They are united in their determination to extend and prolong their domination and exploitation. So we must fight wherever imperialism, neo-colonialism and racialism exist. We too must combine our strength and co-ordinate our strategy in a unified armed struggle. Non-violent methods are now anachronistic in revolution. And so I say to the progressive, revolutionary forces of the world, in the words of Ernesto Ché Guevara: "Let us develop a true proletarian internationalism, with international proletarian armies; the flag under which we fight shall be the sacred cause of redeeming humanity."

It must be understood that liberation movements in Africa, the struggles of Black Power in America or in any other part of the world, can only find consummation in the political unification of Africa, the home of the black man and people of African descent throughout the world. African-Americans have been separated from their cultural and national roots. Black children overseas are not taught of the glory of African civilisation in the history of mankind, of pillaged cities and destroyed tribes. They do not know of the millions of black martyrs who died resisting imperialist aggression. The imperialists and neo-colonialists inside or outside the United States designate everything "good" as "white", and everything "bad" as "black". Black Power says: "We will define ourselves". For centuries, African-Americans have been the victims of racialism. They have now taken up arms to abolish it for ever, and to destroy its fertile breeding ground, the capitalist system. For it is only with the building of a socialist society that peace and racial harmony can be ultimately achieved. It is only world socialism which can provide the solution to the problems of the world today.

For us in Africa, for the people of African descent everywhere, there can be no turning back, no compromise, no fear of failure or death. Africa must and shall fulfil her destiny. Even though revolution in other parts of the world may wither or go astray, the African revolution must reach its goal of unity and socialism. We have taken the correct road, even though hazardous. We face death as we face life with head up, eyes lifted, proud and unafraid. The seed dies that life may come forth. So, we may meet death knowing that we cannot be defeated. For the oppressed peoples of the world will one day triumph. Hundreds and thousands of us have died in many an imperialist war. If we die in the struggle of black emancipation it will be as men bringing into this world the wholesome, rich benefits of Black Power.

And so for us Black Power heralds the long-awaited day of liberation from the shadows of obscurity. We take our place among the peoples of the world without hate or apologies, with confidence and with goodwill towards all men. The spectre of Black Power has taken shape and form and its material presence fights to end the exploitation of man by man.

CONCLUSION

Racial discrimination is the product of an environment, an environment of a divided class society, and its solution is to change that environment. This presupposes the fact that it is only under socialism in the United States of America that the African-American can really be free in the land of his birth.

The Big Lie

AUTHOR'S NOTE

Since the publication of my DARK DAYS IN GHANA, many requests have been received for a separate re-print of Chapter Five, "The Big Lie", to make it more readily available for a wider reading public. My purpose in writing this chapter, the core of the book, was to expose the "big lie" told to the world by the western press that the local reactionaries and neo-colonialists who overthrew the constitutional government of Ghana on 24th February, 1966 acted to save the country from "economic chaos".

The enemies of socialism and the African Revolution struck just as Ghana was on the point of breakthrough in the struggle to achieve economic independence. The First and Second Five Year Development Plans had been successfully implemented, and the Seven Year Development Plan had been launched on 11th March 1964. Barely a month before the "coup" I had formally inaugurated the completed Volta River Project, which was to enable us to develop Ghana's full industrial potential. The great industrial infrastructure had been laid. Ghana was poised for the next phase of the Ghanaian revolution, the establishment of a socialist republic, the principle of which was contained in our 1961 Constitution.

What took place in Ghana in February 1966 must be viewed as part of the world reactionary, counter-revolutionary pattern of armed intervention against socialist-directed, progressive governments. If for a time local reactionaries, imperialists and neo-colonialists appear to achieve some success it can only spur us on to greater effort. Time is on the side of the masses, and nothing can permanently frustrate their ultimate fulfilment.

Conakry.
30th August, 1968.

IT has been said that the fabrication of the "big lie" is essential in the planning of any usurpation of political power. In the case of Ghana, the big lie told to the world was that Ghana needed to be rescued from "economic chaos". Various other lies were hinged to this central lie. The country was said to be hopelessly in debt and the people on the verge of starvation. Among the lies aimed against me personally was the one that I had accumulated a large private fortune; this was to form the basis for an all-out character assassination attempt. But these lies were subsidiary to the one big lie of "economic mismanagement", which was to provide an umbrella excuse for the seizure of power by neo-colonialist inspired traitors.

If Ghana was in such a serious economic condition, why was there no lack of investment in her growing industries? Investors do not put their money into mismanaged enterprises and unstable economies. Why did the imperialist powers try to exert an economic squeeze on Ghana? No

The nurses' training college at Kumasi. Expansion of health services was high on the list of Nkrumah's Government's programme.

one in his right mind bothers to attack an already-dying concern. Who made up the figures of Ghana's supposed "debt"? Why was only one side of the ledger shown—why no mention of assets? How can the obvious evidence of the modernisation and industrialisation of Ghana, such as the new roads, factories, schools and hospitals, the harbour and town of Tema, the Volta and Teffle bridges and the Volta dam be reconciled with the charge of wasted expenditure? If the Ghanaian people were starving, why no evidence of this, and why no popular participation in the "coup"? How was it that Ghana had the highest living standard in Africa per capita, the highest literacy rate, and was the nearest to

A VC10 of Ghana Airways.

achieving genuine economic independence? All these questions, and many related to them, are now being asked. An examination of our development plans and of their implementation reveals the truth—that it was their success and not their failure which spurred our enemies into action. Ghana, on the threshold of economic independence, and in the vanguard of the African revolutionary struggle to achieve continental liberation and unity, was too dangerous an example to the rest of Africa to be allowed to continue under a socialist-directed government.

In the first ten years of its administration, the Ghana government drew up the First and Second Five Year Development Plans (1951-1956 and 1959-1964), and the Consolidation Plan, which covered the two-year gap between these Plans (1957-1959). Under these Plans the foundations were to be laid for the modernisation and industrialisation of Ghana. A skilled labour force was to be trained and an adequate complement of public services built up such as transport, electricity, water and telecommunications.

We had to work fast. Under colonial rule, foreign monopoly interests had tied up our whole economy to suit themselves. We had not a single industry. Our economy was dependent on one cash crop—cocoa. Although our output of cocoa is the largest in the world, there was not a single cocoa processing factory.

Before we took office in 1951 there was no direct railway between Accra and Takoradi, in those days our main port. Passengers and freight had to travel by way of Kumasi. This was because Kumasi was the centre of the timber and mining industries, both of which served foreign interests and were therefore well supplied with the necessary communications. There were few roads, and only a very rudimentary public transport system. For the most part, people walked from place to place. There were very few hospitals, schools or clinics. Most of the villages lacked a piped water supply. In fact, the nakedness of the land when my government began in 1951 has to have been experienced to be believed.

Failure to promote the interests of our people was due to the insatiable demands of colonial exploitation. It was not until we had grasped political

The new port of Tema, the largest artificial harbour in Africa.

power that we were in a position to challenge this, and to develop our resources for the benefit of the Ghanaian people. Those who would judge us merely by the heights we have achieved would do well to remember the depths from which we started.

The condition of Ghana in 1964 showed that our first two Development Plans had been carried out with a high degree of success. We had one of the most modern network of roads in Africa. Takoradi harbour had been extended, and the great artificial harbour at Tema, the largest in Africa, built from scratch. Large extensions to the supply of water, and to the telecommunication network had been constructed, and further extensions were under construction. Our agriculture was being diversified and mechanised. Above all, the Volta River Project, which was designed

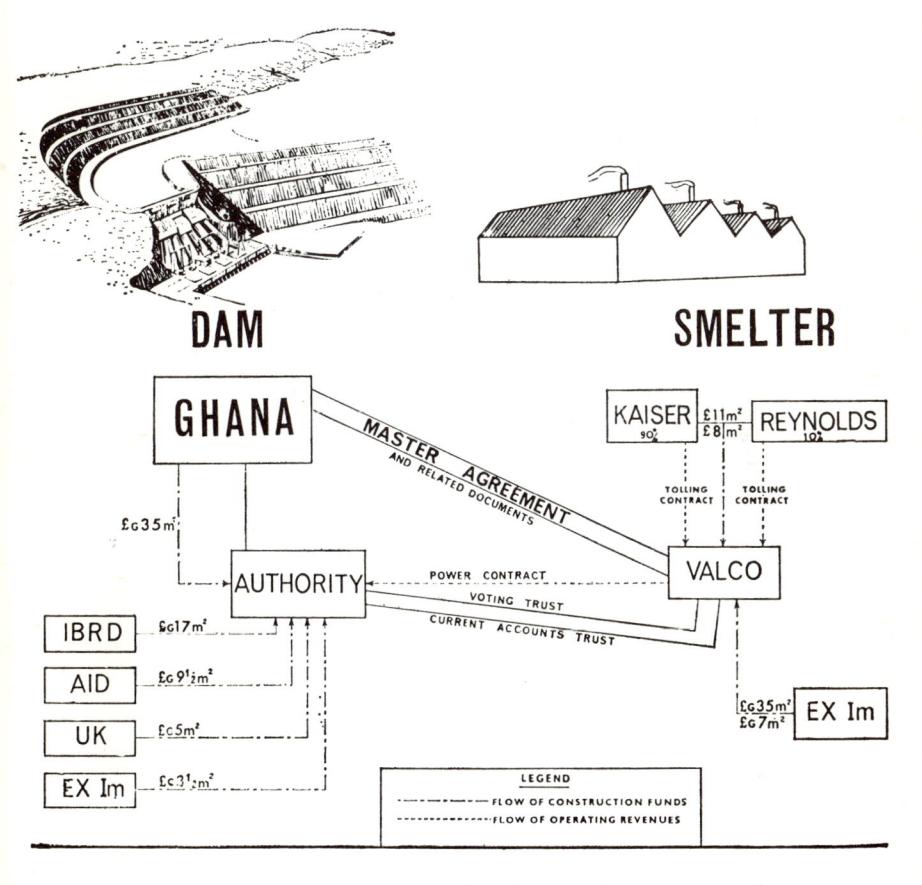

The Volta River Project, providing for the electrification and industrialisation of Ghana.

to provide the electrical power for our great social, agricultural and industrialisation programme, was almost completed.

In education, progress was equally impressive. In ten years we had achieved more than in the whole period of colonial rule. The figures below show the great increase in the numbers of children in primary and middle schools, and of students in secondary and technical schools and in colleges of higher education.

	1951	1961	% Increase
Primary Schools	154,360	481,500	211.9
Middle Schools	66,175	160,000	141.7
Secondary and Technical Schools	3,559	19,143	437.8
Teacher Training Colleges	1,916	4,552	137.5
University Students	208	1,204	478.8

The building of schools and colleges was given top priority in our development plans. We took the unprecedented step in Africa of making all education free, from primary to university level. In addition, text-

The Institute of Ideological Studies at Winneba. Closed down by the NLC. It taught social studies from a socialist viewpoint and researched into the application of socialism to Ghanaian conditions.

books were supplied free to all pupils in primary, middle and secondary schools.

In the 1964-65 school year there were 9,988 primary and middle schools with an enrolment of 1,286,486. There were 89 secondary schools with 32,971 pupils; 47 teacher training colleges with an enrolment of 10,168; 11 technical schools and 3 universities. All this, in a population of 7,500,000 put Ghana in the lead among independent African states. At the same time, a mass literacy campaign has made Ghana the most literate country in the whole of Africa.

A look at some of the other social achievements during the Party's first ten years of office reveals a similar rate of progress.

BASIC SERVICES

	1951	1961	% Increase
Health			
Number of hospital beds	2,368	6,155	159.9
Rural and urban clinics	1	30	—
Doctors and dentists	156	500	220.5
Transport and Communications			
Roads (in miles)—			
Class I (Bitumen)	1,398	2,050	46.7
Class II (Gravel)	2,093	3,346	59.8
(Since 1961 the mileage of motor roads has risen to 19,236. Feeder roads connect most villages to the trunk road network.)			
Post Offices	444	779	75.4
Telephones	7,383	25,488	245.2
Electricity			
Installed electrical capacity (kW)	84,708	120,860	42.7
Electrical power generated (kW '000)	281,983	390,174	38.4

In 1962 the government adopted what was known as the Party's Programme of Work and Happiness. It proclaimed our fundamental objective as the building of a socialist state devoted to the welfare of the masses.

The concrete programme of action for this was worked out in the Seven Year Development Plan launched on 11th March, 1964. In presenting the Plan to the National Assembly I said that its main tasks were first, to speed up the rate of growth of our national economy; secondly, to enable us to embark upon the socialist transformation of our economy through the rapid development of the state and co-operative sectors;

thirdly, to eradicate completely the colonial structure of our economy.

The Plan embodied measures aimed to achieve a self-sustaining economy founded on socialist production and distribution—an economy the people and supporting secondary industries based on the products of our agriculture. Ghana was to be as soon as possible a socialist state. The people, through the state, would have an effective share in the economy of the country and an effective control over it. Thus the principles of scientific socialism would be applied to suit our own particular situation.

The Party has always proclaimed socialism as its objective. But socialism cannot be achieved without socialists, much hard work and sacrifice, and detailed economic planning to provide a vast improvement in the level of material wealth of the country, and distribution of this wealth among the population. It was decided in the Seven Year Plan that Ghana's economy would for the time being remain a mixed one, with a vigorous public and co-operative sector operating alongside the private sector. Our socialist objectives demanded, however, that the public and co-operative sectors should expand faster than the private sector, especially those

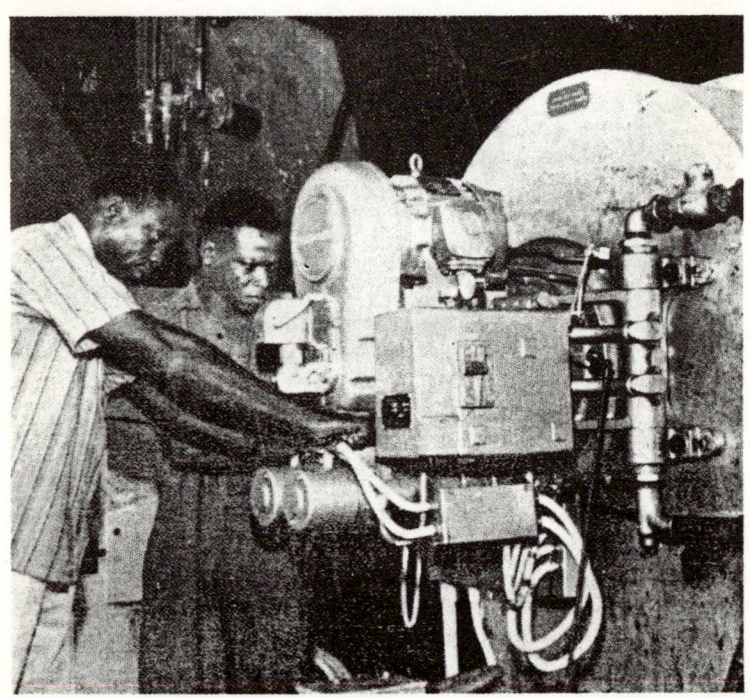

Making soap at Tema. Dozens of factories were built under Nkrumah's industrialisation programme to save the expense of imports and to provide employment to the growing population of Ghana.

strategic areas of production upon which the economy of the country essentially depended.

Various state corporations and enterprises were to be established as a means of securing our economic independence and assisting in the national control of the economy. They were, like all business undertakings, expected to maintain themselves efficiently, and to show profits which could be used for further investment and to help finance public services. A State Management Committee was set up to ensure their efficient and profitable management.

Many state enterprises were quick to show results. The Ghana National Trading Corporation (G.N.T.C.) made a net profit of £4,885,900 in 1965, and had become the largest trading concern in the country. Other state enterprises, by their very nature, took a longer time to develop, and by February 1966 were only just beginning to make a profit. A few, notably in the agricultural sector, were in their infancy and were not expected to yield significant results for some time to come. A certain period of adaptation is necessary for all young industries, particularly in developing countries where the patterns of production are still mainly agricultural and elementary. But it is noteworthy that the traitors of February 1966 found no less than 63 state enterprises which they could put on the market.

Power house at the oil refinery at Tema. Part of the complex of Tema port, industrial estate and residential township, created by the Nkrumah Government.

In our Seven Year Plan we recognised the value of foreign investment in the private sector, particularly in the production of consumer goods, the local processing of Ghanaian raw materials and the utilisation of Ghana's natural resources in the areas of economic activity where a large volume of investment was required. But we welcomed foreign investors in a spirit of partnership. We did not intend to allow them to operate in such a way as to exploit our people. They were to assist in the expansion of our economy in line with our general objectives, an agreed portion of their profits being allocated to promote the welfare and happiness of the Ghanaian people.

The State retained control of the strategic branches of the economy, including public utilities, raw materials, and heavy industry. The state also participated in light and consumer goods industries in which the rates of return on capital were highest. We intended that those industries which provided the basic living needs of the people should be state-owned in order to prevent any exploitation.

It was estimated that during the seven years there would be a total expenditure of £1,016 million. Total government investment in the Plan was to be £476 million. Foreign investors, individual Ghanaians, local authorities and the co-operative sector were expected to invest about £440 million. Ghanaians, it was hoped, would contribute nearly £100 million of direct labour in the construction of buildings, in community development and in the extension of their farms.

Special attention was given to the modernising of agriculture, so that a greater yield and a diversity of crops could be produced. We needed to produce more food locally so that we could reduce our imports of foodstuffs and at the same time improve the health of the people by increasing the protein content in the average diet. Most developing countries face nutritional problems of one kind or another. In our case, the great need was for more fish and meat to provide a properly balanced diet. We planned to increase the output of fish from an estimated 70,000 tons in 1963 to 250,000 tons in 1969. Livestock production, including poultry and eggs, was to increase from 20,080 tons to 37,800 tons.

Immediate steps were taken to expand the fishing fleet and to develop fish processing and marketing facilities. We bought 29 fishing trawlers from Russia. The immense man-made lake formed as part of the Volta River Project was being stocked with fish, and this too was about to bring a big improvement in the diet of the Ghanaian people.

As for meat and poultry, the government subsidised the development of many poultry farms, and the rearing of large herds of cattle. In colonial days, fresh meat, milk and eggs were available to Europeans only.

Before the setback of February 1966, however, they were becoming part of the regular diet of the Ghanaian masses.

The task of correcting the imbalance in our food economy was regarded as the greatest challenge to the agricultural sector of the Plan. Far-reaching schemes were initiated for major improvements in irrigation and water conservation in the Northern and Upper Regions of Ghana. Peasant farmers throughout the country were informed that they would be able to make use of the agricultural machinery of state and co-operative farms. It was not the government's intention to squeeze out the peasant farmer. Far from it, we needed the maximum effort of every individual farmer if we were to achieve our agricultural targets.

During the period of the Plan, Ghana's production of raw materials was to be considerably increased. Cocoa, our main export, earned the country 1,680 million cedis between 1951 and 1961. Of this, the farmers received 1,008 million cedis and the remainder was used by the government and the Cocoa Marketing Board for maintaining public services and for the general development of the country. We increased our cocoa production from 264,000 tons in 1956-57, to 590,000 tons in 1963-64, and huge silos

Work taking place on the construction of the huge power house at the Volta River dam site at Akosombo.

had been built, able to store half the cocoa crop, to enable us to restrict exports and so ensure a fair price for our cocoa in the world market.

Plans were also far advanced to increase exports of timber, and to develop new species of wood for buildings, furniture and other wood products, and for use in paper factories. Efforts were being made to revive our once-flourishing export crop of palm oil. Rubber production was being increased. In the Western Region, a vast new plantation, 18 miles long, had been sown. Within two to three years Ghana was to be one of the greatest rubber producers in Africa. The production of palm oil, cotton, sugar cane and tobacco was being stepped up. By 1970, there were to be four factories in operation producing 100,000 tons of sugar a year, more than sufficient to eliminate the item from our list of imports.

Greatest of all our development projects was the Volta dam. When the Seven Year Plan was launched, the Volta Project was expected to begin to generate electrical power by September 1965. Completion of the Project would enable us to develop the full industrial potential of Ghana. It would increase by nearly 600 per cent the installed electrical capacity of the country. Nearly one-half of this new capacity would be taken up by the aluminium smelter in Tema; it is estimated that Ghana has sufficient bauxite to last for 200 years. But apart from this the Volta Project would have an ample reserve of power for other users, and Ghana would have liberated herself decisively from the possibility of a power shortage becoming a brake on the rate of economic progress.

Construction targets for the various parts of the Volta River Project were achieved, some of them ahead of schedule, and the official inauguration ceremony took place on 23rd January, 1966. At that time, building was about to start on a large subsidiary dam at Bui. Plans were also well advanced for the construction of an alumina plant which would have given Ghanaians control of the whole process of aluminium production. As it was, we were exporting bauxite to the United Kingdom for processing while we were importing alumina manufactured in the United States from bauxite mined in Jamaica for our aluminium smelter.

In keeping with my government's policy of linking Ghana's progress with Africa's total development, provision was made in the Plan for economic co-operation with other African states. As I said in my address to the National Assembly on 11th March 1964:

> "While we wait for the setting up of a Union Government for Africa, we must begin immediately to harmonise our plans for Africa's total development. For example, I see no reason why the independent African states should not, with advantage to each other, join together in an economic union and draw up together a joint Development Plan which will give us greater scope and flexibility to

our mutual advantage. By the same token, I see no reason why the independent African states should not have common shipping and air lines in the interests of improved services and economy. With such rationalisation of our economic policies, we could have common objectives and thus eliminate unnecessary competition and frontier barriers and disputes."

When in fact I inaugurated the completed Volta River Project on 23rd January, 1966, 1 said:

"We are ready and prepared to supply power to our neighbours in Togo, Dahomey, Ivory Coast and Upper Volta. As far as I am concerned this project is not for Ghana alone. Indeed, I have already offered to share our power resources with our sister African states."

On that day at Akosombo, some 60 miles north-east of Accra, when I switched on illuminating lights signifying the official opening of hydro-electric power from the Volta, one of my greatest dreams had come true. I had witnessed the wide-scale electrification of Ghana and the breakthrough into a new era of economic and social advance. The Volta Dam permitted not only a large aluminium plant at Tema processing the

The inauguration of the Volta River Project, 23rd January, 1966.

country's rich bauxite deposits, but a broad range of other industrial projects. The initial power output is 512,000 kW (588,000 kW at full load) and the ultimate power output will be 768,000 kW (882,000 kW at full load). There are 500 miles of transmission lines. The main grid carries 161,000 volts.

The water building up behind the dam is forming the largest man-made lake in the world. It will cover an area of 3,275 square miles with a capacity of 120 million acre feet of water, and will be 250 miles long, with a shore-line of 4,500 miles. Approximately 80,000 people had to be moved from the area submerged by the lake. This necessitated the construction of 50 new villages and towns to accommodate them, the provision of modern housing, schools, piped water, electricity, medical facilities and new forms of employment. Thousands of acres of land had to be cleared, and people settled on farms and smallholdings with up-to-date methods of cultivation and animal husbandry. All this was achieved.

The creation of the Volta Lake has already provided facilities for an important fresh-water fishing industry. The Volta River contained numerous excellent indigenous fish; and research has shown which fish to breed to increase the supply, and how to control weed growth. A number of ports and fishing villages being formed round the lake-side provide bases for a cheap means of transport from the north to the south of Ghana. Furthermore, the lake forms a vast reservoir, making possible the improvement of water supplies to towns and villages and the irrigation of land for agriculture. The natural seasonal fluctuation in the level of the lake will immediately affect 650 square miles of land, permitting the cultivation of rice and other crops. Lake Volta was also to be developed as a holiday and tourist attraction.

Ghanaians are justifiably proud that their own government provided £35,000,000, that is half of the cost of the Volta River Project as well as meeting the cost of the new port and township of Tema, which was an essential part of the scheme. The balance of the £70,000,000 required was to be raised by international loans as follows:

International Bank for Reconstruction and Development	£16,790,000
Agency for International Development of the United States Government	£9,640,000
Export-Import Bank of the United Kingdom Government	£3,570,000
United Kingdom Board of Trade acting for the Export Credits Guarantee Department	£5,000,000

Incidentally, at a time when our detractors talk much of bribery and corruption in the developing countries, it is noteworthy that not a single penny went astray or was misappropriated in the entire Volta undertaking, which involved countless contracts over many years.

Apart from completing the Volta River Project, the Seven Year Development Plan provided for certain further improvements in the physical services. These were mostly intended to improve upon the existing system of transport, communications, water supply and electricity services in order to make them fully capable of supporting the proposed level of industrial and agricultural development.

A considerable proportion of the increase in material wealth that was expected to accrue to the country during the seven years of the Plan's

To show the seriousness with which they regarded the need for African unity the Nkrumah Government built this magnificent complex of buildings in 1965 to house the conference and visiting African leaders.

operation was to be used to promote public welfare services. Education, the health services and housing were all to benefit. As far as health services were concerned, the Plan proposed to change the main orientation which had hitherto been more curative than preventative. Rural health services were developed in such a way that the rate of infant mortality was lowered, and maternity and post-natal care improved. The main cause of poor health in Ghana is the prevalence of endemic diseases such as malaria. The Plan put emphasis on the fight against these endemic diseases.

New regional hospitals, equipped with all specialist facilities were under construction in Tamale, Koforidua, Ho and Sunyani, and existing hospitals were being improved. Arrangements had been made to build six new district hospitals and four more urban polyclinics to assist in the decentralisation of out-patient work. In addition, five new mental hospitals with accommodation for 1,200 patients were designed to be ready by 1970. They were to be backed up by psychiatric units providing treatment for as many mental patients as possible.

The urgent need for more doctors was being met by sending Ghanaian medical students to study abroad, and by the setting up of our own medical school. In 1962, 51 pre-medical students were enrolled at the University of Ghana. When our own medical school is functioning fully it will be empowered to provide a screening system for all doctors trained abroad who wish to practise in Ghana. The medical programme under the Seven Year Development Plan was intended to achieve the following ratios:

1 doctor to 10,000 people
1 nurse to 5,000 patients (including patients in public health centres)
1 technician (laboratory, X-ray, etc.) to 5,000 patients
1 health inspector to 15,000 people
1 health auxiliary (vaccinators, dressing room attendants, etc.) to 1,000 people.

A large network of health centres was being built all over Ghana to serve the rural population, and regional health officers were being provided with training and facilities to enable them to carry out their important work.

The only nursing school which existed in 1945 produced only 8 nurses a year by 1950. In 1961-62 six schools of nursing turned out 265 new nurses and midwives.

Perhaps the most outstanding contribution to public health has come from the Medical Field Unit. This unit was formed to seek out and control trypanosomiasis, and it has been successful in containing the disease. It has also carried out a massive vaccination programme, and played a leading role in the control of epidemics of cerebrospinal meningitis. It is currently actively engaged in combating malaria, leprosy and tuberculosis.

In launching the Seven Year Development Plan, with all its detailed programmes for our country's economic and social progress, I warned about the existence of Ghanaian private enterprise in our midst. It was necessary, I told members of the National Assembly, to distinguish between the two types of business which had grown up within recent years. The first was the type which it was the government's intention to encourage, that of the small businessman who employed his capital in an industry or trade with which he was familiar, and which fulfilled a public need. The second consisted of that class of Ghanaian businesses which were modelled on the old colonial pattern of exploitation. In this category were those who used their capital, not in productive endeavour, but to purchase and resell, at high prices, commodities such as salt, fish and other items of food and consumer goods which were in demand by the people. This type of business served no social purpose, and steps would be taken to see that the nation's banking resources were not used to provide credit for them.

Even more harmful to the economy was another type of enterprise in which some Ghanaians had been participating. This was the setting up of bogus agencies for foreign companies which were in fact nothing

Accra became the centre of Pan-Africanism.

more than organisations for distributing bribes and for exerting improper pressures on behalf of foreign companies. The government intended to carry out a thorough investigation into the activities of these agencies and to suppress them.

The initiative of Ghanaian businessmen would not be cramped, but we intended to take steps to see that is was channelled towards desirable social ends and was not expended in the exploitation of the community. We would discourage anything which threatened our socialist objectives.

For this reason, no Ghanaian would be allowed to take up shares in any enterprise under foreign investment. Instead, our people would be encouraged to save by investing in the state sector and in co-operative undertakings.

This, in essence, was our Seven Year Development Plan, a Plan scientifically worked out with the participation of some of the world's leading experts on economic and social planning. It was to integrate educational, industrial and agricultural programmes to bring full employment and to make possible the achievement of economic independence and a big rise in our living standards. And this was the Plan the rebel military regime scrapped as soon as it usurped power.

No possible justification can be given for its abandonment and the sell-out of Ghana's increasing assets. The first phase of the Plan was going well, and according to schedule. During the first year, £48,900,000 was spent on development projects, and of this amount, £16 million went into the key sectors, agriculture and industry. In agriculture, the emphasis was on diversification. State farms cultivated 24,000 acres of rubber, oil palm, banana, urena, lobata, coconut and citrus. Together with the agricultural wing of the Workers Brigade, which alone had 12,500 acres, the two institutions cultivated large areas for cereals and vegetables. During this period also, improvements were made in the modernisation and productivity of private and co-operative farms.

In the industrial sphere, during this period, nearly all the initiative was in the public sector. The construction of many new industrial plants

Women members of the Workers' Brigade making pillows and mattresses in one of their own factories.

were undertaken. These included a steelworks (30,000 tons), two cocoa processing plants, one at Takoradi (28,000 tons) and the other at Tema (68,600 tons), two sugar refineries, a textile printing plant, a glass factory, a chocolate factory, a meat processing plant, a radio assembly plant and a large printing works at Tema. All these factories were brought into production during the first phase of the Plan.

In addition, work was well advanced on a textile mill and a complex of food industries at Tema, a gold refinery at Tarkwa, and asbestos, cement, shoe and rubber-tyre factories at Kumasi. The buildings for an atomic reactor at Kwabinya were almost finished. So also was a plant for the manufacture of pre-fabricated houses. In fact, the basic policy underlying the Seven Year Development Plan, to change the structure of our mainly agricultural economy into a balanced modern economy, was going ahead with great speed and efficiency. We were successfully managing to use our local raw materials for establishing industries, and were beginning to satisfy local demand for certain consumer goods. For example, we produced matches, shoes, nails, sweets, chocolate, soft drinks, whisky, beer, gin, etc., cigarettes, biscuits, paints, canned fruit, insecticides and other chemicals. An indication of the build-up of our industrial strength may be seen in the fact that at the beginning of January 1966 imports of raw materials amounted to about 9 per cent of Ghana's total imports.

Before the February action, the government was investing £25 million annually in manufacturing projects, and the country's main exports:

Cocoa	680	million cedis annually
Timber	31.2	,, ,, ,,
Minerals	48	,, ,, ,,

were providing a sound basis for profitable industrial enterprise.

On an average, Ghana anually imports about 264 million cedis of semi-finished and finished products consisting mainly of food and drinks, textiles and clothing, construction materials and capital equipment. Annual exports average some 254.4 million cedis of primary produce, mainly cocoa, timber, gold, diamonds and manganese. Our growing industries were to make possible a cut in imports, particularly of consumer goods, and an increase in our exports, not only of primary produce but of our own locally-manufactured products.

A look at the orientation of Ghana's investment policy during recent years throws further light on the direction in which Ghana was moving. In 1951-1959, 90 per cent (i.e. £127.8 million) of governing expenditure was allocated to provide social services and to create the infrastructure of economic growth, while 10 per cent (£13.4 million) went to the productive sector. During the 1951-1962 period, an average amount of £15.5

million was allocated yearly to the public sector during the First Development Plan, and during the Consolidated Plan an average of £21.4 million yearly. Under the Second Development Plan an average amount of £50 million yearly went to the public sector. Under the Seven Year Development plan an average of £68 million was going to the public sector yearly, representing a total investment of £442 million for development projects

A jute bag factory producing millions of cocoa sacks that previously had to be imported.

belonging to the public sector. To the above-mentioned £68 million, £34 million were added for the Volta complex—in all £476 million for the public sector.

Investments during the Seven Year Development Plan period (1964-1970) were therefore distributed between social services and infrastructure (62%) and the directly productive sector (38%). This represented for Ghanaians an investment of £10 per head, per year (to be compared with the maximum investment of 8 shillings per head, per year, in countries associated with the Common Market during the 1958-1962 period). It may also be noted that Ghana has a 240 cedis per capita income, that is to say, practically the highest in independent Africa—and in real terms, the highest in Africa, since it cannot be considered that the distribution of gross national product is equitable in countries like South Africa, Rhodesia and most of the neo-colonialist states.

The qualitative aspect of Ghana's imports reveals that while consumer goods dropped from one-half of total imports in 1961 to two-fifths in

Fishing co-operatives were formed so that fishermen could, with Government assistance, buy motorised vessels and at Sekondi the Nkrumah Government set up its own yards for building motorised fishing boats.

1963, industrial equipment and goods increased from 50.6 per cent of total imports in 1961 to 60.6 per cent in 1963.

On the question of ownership, it is worth noting that in 1965 the State controlled between 60 per cent and 65 per cent of the national production (this percentage was to rise in 1970), and that since 1963, the total gold and foreign exchange assets of Ghana, and total capital exports, were under state financial control.

Apart from a 41 per cent control over consumer goods imports, the State was controlling in 1965 over 60 per cent of the exports in the most important sectors such as gold, diamonds, cocoa. In the case of timber, the Timber Marketing Board had increased its foreign exchange earnings from £5.7 million in 1962 to £8 million in 1964, and was able during the same period, to grant revolving loans of £2 million to Ghanaian producers organised into co-operatives.

When the Party came to power in 1951, all imported goods were in the hands of a few big foreign firms, especially the monopolist United Africa Company, part of the Unilever complex. Foreign firms dominated Ghana's trade and virtually controlled the economy. By 1965, however, the grip was being broken. The nationalised Ghana National Trading Corporation was distributing 32 per cent of all imports.

My government was also breaking through the stranglehold of the big international banking houses. In 1958, foreign banks held one-third of Ghana's foreign currency reserves; in 1965 they held none.

Our success in breaking the web of economic control which Western capitalism has imposed across the whole of the African continent, and our clear socialist policies, provoked the hostility of the imperialist powers. They knew that as long as I was alive and at the head of the Party in

One of the many factories set up by the Nkrumah Government.

Ghana the process could not be halted and neo-colonialist exploitation could not be re-imposed. Ours was a system they could neither penetrate nor manipulate.

Significantly, one of the first acts of the "N.L.C." was to announce the abandonment of the Seven Year Development Plan, which would have given the Ghanaian people the only worthwhile independence—real economic independence. The "N.L.C." replaced it with a two-year "review period" during which the socialised industries would be dismantled and the door opened once more to unrestricted "private enterprise"—in fact, they were establishing a neo-colonialist economic subjugation of Ghana.

The only Ghanaians to benefit from such a sell-out were the African middle-class hangers-on to neo-colonialist privilege and the neo-colonialist trading firms. For the mass of workers, peasants and farmers, the victims of the capitalist free-for-all, it meant a return to the position of "drawers of water and hewers of wood" to Western capitalism.

Of course, the Ghanaian economy was not without its problems, but is this not true of all national economies, and particularly those of developing countries in the context of the growing gap between rich and poor nations? In any event, these difficulties were not determinant. It was no mean achievement that in January 1965, after five years as a Republic, Ghana had 63 state enterprises and a budget of £200 million, including a supplementary budget, for its population of nearly eight million; while

Accra's Ring Road. Before Nkrumah's Government this area was flooded everytime it rained. Since 1961 the mileage of motor roads built by the Nkrumah Government had risen to 19,236.

Nigeria, richer in national resources and with a population of 55 million, had a budget of £78 million.

Imperialist circles have talked much about Ghana's external debt, given as £250 million. Apart from the dubious accounting which arrived at this conveniently round sum, a figure such as this means nothing unless it is set in the context of the overall Ghanaian economic situation. To implement our various Development Plans it was necessary to borrow considerable sums of money, but it was borrowed on the basis of building capital assets such as the Volta dam, and over 100 industries established

The Young Pioneers banned by the NLC. The Nkrumah Government had given young people the inspiration of taking part in the work of national reconstruction.

in Ghana since independence. The government made sure that the international agreements signed were based on economic feasibility, and that the money borrowed could create something lasting and beneficial not only for us in our lifetime but for the generations to follow. Seen in the light of Ghana's growing industries and increasing exports, her "indebtedness" is put in proper perspective—as an index of the investors' confidence in the enterprise and the management they helped to finance. In addition, it should be noted that only some £20 million was due to be paid in 1967, and this did not prevent the government from refusing the political conditions attached to a loan from the International Monetary Fund (I.M.F.)

Long faces are pulled at the drop in our foreign reserves since independence. In 1957, Ghana had a sterling balance of £200 million. This has not been "squandered" as the imperialist press would have its readers believe. It has been used to pay off succesive balance of payments deficits due to the rise in prices of imported consumer goods, and the drastic fall in the price of our main export crop—cocoa. It should be remembered that the sterling balance was in fact a forced loan at negligible interest which Britain acquired from Ghana during and after the Second World War. Its accumulation was made possible by the Cocoa Marketing Board which prevented Ghanaian cocoa growers from receiving the bulk of the proceeds from the sale of their cocoa. The capital the growers might have amassed from cocoa profits and later might have invested in industry was locked up in London "to maintain the confidence of the foreign investor".

Our imperialist critics would be better employed examining the economic situation in their own countries, many of which are in grave financial difficulties. In Britain, for example, the £1 is devalued, there is a continuous "balance of payments crisis" and unemployment is a serious problem.

In Ghana, before 24th February 1966, unemployment was virtually unknown. All salaries were regularly paid and new jobs were constantly being created as the Seven Year Development Plan was being implemented. It was estimated that more than one million new workers would be needed to fill the new jobs which would be created, and also to replace those who left the labour force during the Plan period. More than 500,000 of them would be employed in industry and agriculture, and another 400,000 would be needed in government services, commerce and construction. The remainder were to be employed in transport, mining and the public utility services. In fact, plans were being made to import labour.

When neo-colonialist inspired traitors seized power in February 1966, we were expanding our educational system to provide the necessary numbers of qualified people to meet these new demands. Changes were made to shorten and to improve educational courses. For example, there was a reduction made in the number of school years so that University graduates would be ready for employment at the age of 21 or 22 instead of 24 or 25 as used to be the case. Under the new plan, the time spent in middle school was reduced by two years and the secondary school period by one year. Primary education took six years and was followed by two years of vocationally oriented training for those who did not intend to proceed to secondary schools. The reduction by two years of the ten-year middle school programme was designed to permit 300,000 additional young people to join the labour force during the seven-year period, and to equip them with basic training in technical and agricultural skills.

The figures below illustrate the planned growth in school enrolment 1963-1970:

	Total enrolment	
	1963	1970
Primary—Middle	1,200,000	2,200,000
Secondary	23,000	78,000
Teacher Training	6,000	21,000
Technical Schools	4,000	6,000
Clerical Training	100	5,000
Universities	2,000	5,000

The intake would be such that from 1968 nearly 250,000 children would complete primary-middle school and 20,000 others would leave secondary school each year. For the entire Plan period, the output from all educational institutions was to have been approximately as follows:

Middle and continuing schools	750,000
Secondary schools	46,000
Universities	9,000
Technical schools	14,000
Secretarial schools	11,000
Teacher training	31,000

The tremendous rate of our educational growth created certain difficulties. We needed many more trained teachers, and more school and college buildings. We were successfully overcoming these problems. The government allocated 153.6 million cedis (£64 million) for the construction of post-primary school buildings to feed the new secondary and higher educational institutions. The University of Ghana, the Kwame Nkrumah University of Science and Technology, and Cape Coast University College were supplying a large number of teachers; and expatriate teachers had been recruited to fill other vacancies until our own output of teachers was sufficient to cope with the demand. The Cape Coast University College was to have become a fully-fledged University in September 1966, but the "N.L.C." has abandoned the plan.

Local authorities and individual communities were primarily responsible for the provision of elementary school facilities, though the government provided teachers, textbooks and other services for primary schools. Special subsidies were given to less favoured parts of the country to help in the development of primary education.

To assist in solving the manpower problem, the Trades Union Congress, the Ministry of Labour and employers' associations launched and rapidly expanded in-service training schemes to augment the knowledge and technical skill of all new employees. Adult education facilities were also being improved to provide part-time and evening classes for craftsmen, foremen, technicians and managers. The Institute of Public Education, the Workers' College, the Universities and other specialised institutions were redoubling their efforts to make this type of education available throughout the country.

Ghana was going ahead. The nation's economy was almost completely controlled by Ghanaians, and our educational planning was producing educated and skilled personnel to meet the demand. Likewise, thoroughgoing machinery had been established for the political education of the masses so that our socialist objectives, and Ghana's role in the wider African revolution, might be clearly understood. This was the purpose of the Young Pioneers, the T.U.C. educational programme, and the Ideological Institute of Winneba where cadres were being trained. It was to make possible the unfolding of the next phase of the Ghanaian revolution: the establishment of a socialist republic, the principle of which was enshrined in the 1961 Constitution of the Republic of Ghana.

This process was well on its way when in 1965, the imperialists and neo-colonialists stepped up their pressure on Ghana in the form of an economic squeeze. In that year, the price of cocoa on the world market was artificially forced down from £476 in 1954 to £87 10s. a ton (1965). This meant that although Ghana exported 500,000 tons of cocoa, she earned only £77 million, or less than her receipts in the mid-1950's for 250,000 tons.

When the Seven Year Development Plan was drawn up, it was assumed that the price of cocoa on the world market would be at least £200 a ton. This was not an unreasonable assumption. Between 1953 and 1963, prices fell only once below £190 a ton. In 1954 the price was £476, and in 1957-58 it was £352. But the very year the Seven Year Development Plan was launched, cocoa prices began to fall steeply. At the same time, the prices of capital and manufactured goods needed for industrial and agricultural projects under the Plan were rapidly rising. Between 1950 and 1961 they had risen by over 25 per cent.

In 1964, the imperialist powers, the principal consumers of cocoa, promised at the Geneva meeting of the United Nations Conference on Trade and Development (U.N.-C.T.A.D.) that they would "lift barriers in the form of tariffs and duties on primary products, either raw, processed or semi-processed". This would have meant that cocoa-grindings, cocoa butter and chocolate products whose price was firm, could have been sold in the metropolitan markets to cushion the effects of the low cocoa prices. But Britain and the U.S.A. did not keep their promise to lower trade barriers against processed and semi-processed primary products. Ghana, regarded by them as a pace-setter in Africa, could not be allowed to succeed in building socialism.

When I spoke to the Ghana cocoa farmers on 22nd September 1965, I drew attention to the breach of faith of the cocoa consumers and said that if tariff walls prevented us from selling our chocolate abroad we could still sell it in Ghana and in other African countries at a price well within the means of all. I announced that cocoa powder was being distributed to schoolchildren, and that the production of cocoa butter, in demand for the manufacture of cosmetics and pharmaceuticals, was being expanded.

We constructed silos which, when completed, would enable us to withhold more than half of our cocoa crop from the world market. This amount would be more than the combined world cocoa surplus of production over consumption. We were, in fact, breaking through the cocoa price squeeze. The U.S.A., however, was stockpiling a record quantity of cocoa to be used to keep prices down. In its 1966 Commodity Review, the United Nations Food and Agricultural Organisation (F.A.O.), reported that the total stocks of cocoa beans in consuming countries at the end of 1964 amounted to 500,000 tons, and that by December 1965 this total was further increased.

The U.S.A. and Britain could, if they had wanted, have fixed a reasonable price for cocoa and so have eased the economic situation in Ghana. They had no wish to do so. On the contrary, the forcing down of the price of cocoa was part of their policy of preparing the economic ground for political action in the form of a "coup" and a change of government.

Throughout 1965, and before then, the U.S. government exerted various other forms of economic pressure on Ghana. It withheld investment and credit guarantees from potential investors, put pressure on existing providers of credit to the Ghanaian economy, and negated applications for loans made by Ghana to American-dominated financial institutions such as the I.M.F.

This pressure ended smartly after 24th February 1966 when the U.S. State Department's political objective had been achieved. The price of cocoa suddenly rose on the world market, and the I.M.F. rushed to the aid of the "N.L.C."

If further proof were needed of America's political motives it may be seen in the U.S. government's hysterical reaction to the publication of my book, *Neo-Colonialism—The Last Stage of Imperialism* in October 1965. In this book I exposed the economic stranglehold exercised by foreign monopolistic complexes such as the Anglo-American Corporation, and illustrated the ways in which this financial grip perpetuated the paradox of Africa: poverty in the midst of plenty. The American Government sent me a note of protest, and promptly refused Ghana $35 million of "aid".

The fact that our enemies decided finally on subversion and violence as the only effective way in which to achieve their objective of halting the Ghanaian revolution and bringing Ghana into the neo-colonalist fold, is a measure of the success of our economic policies. We had proved that we were strong enough to develop independently, not only without foreign tutelage, but also in the context of active imperialist and neo-colonialist resistance.

The Myth of the 'Third World'

First published in "Labour Monthly", October 1968.

THERE is much loose talk and woolly writing about the so-called Third World. To some it means all the developing nations; to some it suggests the coloured peoples of the world; others think of it as referring to a vague, amorphous mass of uncommitted peoples, the oppressed and exploited of the earth who are neither "east" nor "west" but who are a kind of third, neutral force in the world.

To Franz Fanon, the "Third World" clearly meant the colonies and ex-colonies, and in his book "The Wretched of the Earth" he makes a specific case study of the problems of decolonisation. For him, the "wretched" are those who have suffered the oppression and exploitation of colonialism. "The Third World is not cut off from the rest. Quite the contrary, it is at the middle of the whirlpool", and is characterised by "neutralism". Its people are committed to a non-capitalist road, since capitalist exploitation is their enemy. But the "Third World" should refuse to become a factor in the fierce competition which exists between the capitalist and socialist systems, and ought "to find their own particular values and methods and a style which shall be peculiar to them".

Fanon did not mean non-commitment or non-alignment in the commonly-accepted sense, though both have come to be associated with the term. The very mention of the "Third World" suggests to some a kind of passivity, a non-participation, an opting out of the conflict between the two worlds of capitalism and socialism.

It is this concept which seems to have led to most of the misuse of the term "Third World", and renders its use so misleading. There is no middle road between capitalism and socialism.

Two questions must be asked. First, does a "Third World" really exist? Secondly, is it possible, either in terms of ideology or practical politics, in the ever-sharpening conflict between revolutionary and counter-revolutionary forces in the world to adopt a position of neutrality or non-alignment?

Clearly, the "Third World" is not definable on a racial or colour basis, though in fact most of the oppressed peoples are non-white. Is it then the apparently uncommitted or non-aligned who form the "Third World"?

The expression first came to be widely used when two Conferences of Non-Aligned States had been held. The first was in Belgrade in 1961. There were 25 participating states and three observer countries. The cold war and nuclear arms race was at its height and there seemed a very real possibility that the world might be plunged into a war which would mean the end of civilisation as we know it. The main purpose of the Conference, therefore, was to employ all the efforts of the participating countries to bring about the destruction of nuclear stockpiles and to divert the vast scientific and technological resources at the disposal of the great powers to positive and progressive channels.

The Second Conference of Non-Aligned States was held in Cairo in October 1964. There were then 46 participating states and ten observer countries. Non-alignment seemed to be practical politics. In my address at that Conference I said:

> "We are all here as Non-Aligned nations but the term 'Non-Aligned' as applied to us has not yet covered every form of policy which it connotes. We came into existence as a protest and a revolt against the state of affairs in international relations caused by the division of the world into opposing blocs of east and west. We came into existence as a revolt against imperialism and neo-colonialism which are also the basic cause of world tension and insecurity."

I went on to say that these states which claimed to be non-aligned had the right to choose the political and economic philosophy which was considered the most suitable for their rapid development and advancement. The fact that Ghana accepted socialism did not necessarily imply opposition to any other country or people. "Socialism", I said, "does not belong to the Soviet Union or China, or for that matter to any other country; it is an international idea."

Many of us thought at that time that it was the duty of the Non-Aligned States to assert their full weight against the senseless build-up of nuclear weapons which threatened the whole world. With "east" and "west", two power blocs of roughly equal strength, poised it seemed on the brink of nuclear warfare, there appeared to be reprieve for the world only in the holding of a balance of power by some third force which would prevent either of the two sides from starting a major war.

After the First Conference, Pandit Nehru and I went to Moscow on behalf of the Non-Aligned States, and President Modibo Keita of Mali and President Sukarno of Indonesia went to Washington.

Although there was no sudden and dramatic lessening of world tension as a result of these missions, the threat of nuclear warfare has to some extent lessened.

However, in the present world situation, with the armed phase of the revolutionary struggle well-launched in Africa, Asia and Latin America, and in the USA itself by the Black Power Movement, it is no longer possible to adopt a third position outside the main conflict. The world struggle, and the cause of world tension, has to be seen not in the old political context of the cold war, that is, of nation states and power blocs, but in terms of revolutionary and counter-revolutionary peoples. It cuts right across territorial boundaries and has nothing to do with colour or race. It is a war to the finish between the oppressed and the oppressors, between those who pursue a capitalist path, and those committed to socialist policies.

Yet old beliefs die hard. Although non-alignment is an anachronism, there are still a few politicians and heads of state who cling to the idea of neutralism and who advocate the holding of more Conferences of Non-Aligned States. Their thinking is a form of political escapism—a reluctance to face the stark realities of the present situation.

The oppressed and exploited peoples are the struggling revolutionary masses committed to the socialist world. Some of them are not yet politically aware. Others are very much aware, and are already engaged in the armed liberation struggle. At whatever stage they have reached in their resistance to exploitation and oppression, they belong to the permanent socialist revolution. They do not constitute a "Third World". They are part of the revolutionary upsurge which is everywhere challenging the capitalist, imperialist and neo-colonialist power structure of reaction and counter-revolution. There are thus two worlds only, the revolutionary and the counter-revolutionary world — the socialist world trending towards communism, and the capitalist world with its extensions of imperialism, colonialism and neo-colonialism.

Today then, the "Third World" is neither a practical political concept nor a reality. It is merely a misused expression which has come to mean everything and nothing. It has been used with equal looseness both by those committed to the revolutionary struggle and by those who are its deadly enemies. The western press has gladly made use of it to serve its own ends by associating it with racism, and by equating it with concepts such as non-alignment, neutralism and co-existence. It has thus helped to prevent the full weight of the so-called "Third World" being identified openly and decisively as part of the socialist world.

If we are to achieve revolutionary socialism then we must avoid any suggestion that will imply that there is any separation between the socialist world and a "Third World."

Misused and misleading political terms must be either abandoned or defined clearly. Where the revolutionary struggle is in the armed phase as in Africa, Asia and Latin America, it is particularly important that there should be the utmost clarity of political expression.

The purpose of an article I wrote in 1966 under the title "African Socialism Revisited" published in African Forum, Vol. 1, No. 3, was to show that there is no such thing as "African Socialism". The term had come to be employed as proof of the existence of brands of socialism peculiar to Africa, such as Arab socialism, pragmatic socialism, and this or that socialism, when in fact there is only one true socialism: scientific socialism.

I do not deny the existence of the struggling "wretched of the earth", but maintain that they do not exist in isolation, as the "Third World". They are an integral part of the revolutionary world, and are committed to the hilt in the struggle against capitalism to end the exploitation of man by man.

"African Socialism" Revisited

(Reprint of an article in "African Forum", Vol. 1, No. 3, 1966)

THE term "socialism" has become a necessity in the platform diction and political writings of African leaders. It is a term which unites in the recognition that the restoration of Africa's humanist and egalitarian principles of society calls for socialism. All of us, therefore, even though pursuing widely contrasting policies in the task of reconstructing our various nation-states, still use "socialism" to describe our respective efforts. The question must therefore be faced: What real meaning does the term retain in the context of contemporary African politics? I warned about this in my book "Consciencism" (Paperback, Panaf Books, 1970, p. 105):

"And yet, socialism in Africa today tends to lose its objective content in favour of a distracting terminology and in favour of a general confusion. Discussion centres more on the various conceivable types of socialism than upon the need for socialist development".

Some African political leaders and thinkers certainly use the term "socialism" as it should in my opinion be used: to describe a complex of social purposes and the consequential social and economic policies, organisational pattterns, state structure, and ideologies which can lead to the attainment of those purposes. For such leaders, the aim is to remould African society in the socialist direction; to reconsider African society in such a manner that the humanism of traditional African life reasserts itself in a modern technical community. Consequently, socialism in Africa introduces a new social synthesis in which modern technology is reconciled with human values, in which the advanced technical society is realised without the staggering social malefactions and deep schisms of capitalist industrial society. For true economic and social development cannot be promoted without the real socialisation of productive and distributive processes. Those African leaders who believe these principles are the socialists in Africa.

There are, however, other African political leaders and thinkers who use the term "socialism" because they believe that socialism would, in the words of Chandler Morse, "smooth the road to economic development." It becomes necessary for them to employ the term in a "charismatic effort to rally support" for the policies that do not really promote economic and social development. Those African leaders who believe these principles are supposed to be the "African socialists."

It is interesting to recall that before the split in the Second International, Marxism was almost indistinguishable from social democracy. Indeed, the German Social Democratic Party was more or less the guardian of the doctrine of Marxism, and both Marx and Engels supported that Party. Lenin, too, became a member of the Social Democratic Party. After the break-up of the Second International, however, the meaning of the term "social democracy" altered, and it became possible to draw a real distinction between socialism and social democracy. A similar situation has arisen in Africa. Some years ago, African political leaders and writers used the term "African socialism" in order to label the concrete forms that socialism might assume in Africa. But the realities of the diverse and irreconcilable social, political and economic policies being pursued by African states today have made the term "African socialism" meaningless and irrelevant. It appears to be much more closely associated with anthropology than with political economy. "African socialism" has now come to acquire some of its greatest publicists in Europe and North America precisely because of its predominant anthropological charm. Its foreign publicists include not only the surviving social democrats of Europe and North America, but other intellectuals and liberals who themselves are dyed in the wool of social democracy. It was no accident, let me add, that the 1962 Dakar Colloquium made such capital of "African socialism"; but the uncertainties concerning the meaning and specific policies of "African socialism" have led some of us to abandon the term because it fails to express its original meaning and because it tends to obscure our fundamental socialist commitment.

Today, the phrase "African socialism" seems to espouse the view that the traditional African society was a classless society imbued with the spirit of humanism and to express a nostalgia for that spirit. Such a conception of socialism makes a fetish of the communal African society. But an idyllic, African classless society (in which there were no rich and no poor) enjoying a drugged serenity is certainly a facile simplification; there is no historical or even anthropological evidence for any such a society. I am afraid the realities of African society were somewhat more sordid.

All available evidence from the history of Africa, up to the eve of the European colonisation, shows that African society was neither classless nor devoid of a social hierarchy. Feudalism existed in some parts of

Africa before colonisation; and feudalism involves a deep and exploitative social stratification, founded on the ownership of land. It must also be noted that slavery existed in Africa before European colonisation, although the earlier European contact gave slavery in Africa some of its most vicious characteristics. The truth remains, however, that before colonisation, which became widespread in Africa only in the nineteenth century, Africans were prepared to sell, often for no more than thirty pieces of silver, fellow tribesmen and even members of the same "extended" family and clan. Colonialism deserves to be blamed for many evils in Africa, but surely it was not preceded by an African Golden Age or paradise. A return to the pre-colonial African society is evidently not worthy of the ingenuity and efforts of our people.

All this notwithstanding, one could still argue that the basic organisation of many African societies in different periods of history manifested a certain communalism and that the philosophy and humanist purposes behind that organisation are worthy of recapture. A community in which each saw his well-being in the welfare of the group certainly was praiseworthy, even if the manner in which the well-being of the group was pursued makes no contribution to our purposes. Thus, what socialist thought in Africa must recapture is not the structure of the "traditional African society" but its spirit, for the spirit of communalism is crystallised in its humanism and in its reconciliation of individual advancement with group welfare. Even if there is incomplete anthropological evidence to reconstruct the "traditional African society" with accuracy, we can still recapture the rich human values of that society. In short, an anthropological approach to the "traditional African society" is too much unproven; but a philosophical approach stands on much firmer ground and makes generalisation feasible.

One predicament in the anthropological approach is that there is some disparity of view concerning the manifestations of the "classlessness" of the "traditional African society". While some hold that the society was based on the equality of its members, others hold that it contained a hierarchy and division of labour in which the hierarchy—and therefore power—was founded on spiritual and democratic values. Of course, no society can be founded on the equality of its members, although some societies are founded on egalitarianism, which is something quite different. Similarly, a classless society that at the same time rejoices in a hierarchy of power (as distinct from authority) must be accounted a marvel of socio-political finesse.

We know that the "traditional African society" was founded on principles of egalitarianism. In its actual workings, however, it had various shortcomings. Its humanist impulse, nevertheless, is something that continues to urge us toward our all-African socialist reconstruction. We postulate each man to be an end in himself, not merely a means; and we accept the necessity of guaranteeing each man equal opportunities for his development. The implications of this socio-political practice have to be worked out scientifically, and the necessary social and economic policies pursued with resolution. Any meaningful humanism must begin from egalitarianism and must lead to objectively chosen policies for safeguarding and sustaining egalitarianism. Hence, socialism. Hence, also, scientific socialism.

A further difficulty that arises from the anthropological approach to socialism, or "African socialism" is the glaring division between existing African societies and the communalistic society that was. I warned in my book "Consciencism" that "our society is not the old society, but a new society enlarged by Islamic and Euro-Christian influences". This is a fact that any socio-economic policies must recognise and take into account. Yet the literature of "African socialism" comes close to suggesting that today's African societies are communalistic. The two societies are not conterminous, and such an equation cannot be supported by any attentive observation. It is true that this disparity is acknowledged in some of the literature of "African socialism"; thus, my friend and colleague Julius Nyerere, in acknowledging the disequilibrium between what was and what is in terms of African societies, attributes the differences to the importations of European colonialism.

We know, of course, that the defeat of colonialism and even neo-colonialism will not result in the automatic disappearance of the imported patterns of thought and social organisation. For those patterns have taken root, and are in varying degrees sociological features of our contemporary society. Nor will a simple return to the communalistic society of ancient Africa offer a solution either. To advocate a return, as it were, to the rock from which we were hewn is a charming thought, but we are faced with contemporary problems, which have arisen from political subjugation, economic exploitation, educational and social backwardness, increases in population, familiarity with the methods and products of industrialisation, modern agricultural techniques. These—as well as a host of other complexities—can be resolved by no mere communalistic society, however sophisticated, and anyone who so advocates must be caught in insoluble dilemmas of the most excruciating kind. All available evidence from socio-political history discloses that such a return to a *status quo ante* is quite unexampled in the evolution of societies. There is, indeed, no theoretical or historical reason to indicate that it is at all possible.

When one society meets another, the observed historial trend is that acculturation results in a balance of forward movement, a movement in which each society assimilates certain useful attributes of the other. Social evolution is a dialectical process; it has ups and downs, but, on balance, it always represents an upward trend.

Islamic civilisation and European colonialism are both historical experiences of the traditional African society, profound experiences that have permanently changed the complexion of the traditional African society. They have introduced new values and a social, cultural, and economic organisation into African life. Modern African societies are not traditional, even if backward, and they are clearly in a state of socio-economic disequilibrium. They are in this state because they are not anchored to a steadying ideology.

The way out is certainly not to regurgitate all Islamic or Euro-colonial influences in a futile attempt to recreate a past that cannot be resurrected. The way out is only forward, forward to a higher and reconciled form of society, in which the quintessence of the human purposes of traditional African society reasserts itself in a modern context—forward, in short, to socialism, through policies that are scientifically devised and correctly applied. The inevitability of a forward way out is felt by all; thus, Leopold Sedor Senghor, although favouring some kind of return to African communalism, insists that the refashioned African society must accommodate the "positive contribution" of colonial rule, "such as the economic and technical infrastructure and the French education system". The economic and technical infrastructure of even French colonialism and the French educational system must be assumed, though this can be shown to be imbued with a particular socio-political philosophy. This philosophy, as should be known, is not compatible with the philosophy underlying communalism, and the desired accommodation would prove only a socio-political mirage.

Senghor has, indeed, given an account of the nature of the return to Africa. His account is highlighted by statements using some of his own words: that the African is "a field of pure sensation"; that he does not measure or observe, but "lives" a situation; and that this way of acquiring "knowledge" by confrontation and intuition is "Negro African", the acquisition of knowledge by reason, "Hellenic". In "African Socialism" (London and New York, 1964, pp. 72-73), he proposes that we

"consider the Negro-African as he faces the Other: God, man, animal, tree or pebble, natural or social phenomenon. In contrast to the classic European, the Negro-African does not draw a line between himself and the object, he does not hold it at a distance, nor does he merely look at it and analyse it. After holding it at a distance, after scanning it without analysing it, he takes it vibrant in his hands, careful not to kill or fix it. He touches it, feels, it, smells it. The Negro-African is like one of those Third Day Worms, a pure field of sensations . . . Thus the Negro-African sympathises, abandons his personality to become identified with the Other, dies to be reborn in the Other. He does not assimilate; he is assimilated. He lives a common life with the Other; he lives in a symbiosis".

It is clear that socialism cannot be founded on this kind of metaphysics of knowledge.

To be sure, there is a connection between communalism and socialism. Socialism stands to communalism as capitalism stands to slavery. In socialism, the principles underlying communalism are given expression in modern circumstances. Thus, whereas communalism in a non-technical society can be laissez-faire, in a technical society where sophisticated means of production are at hand, the situation is different; for if the underlying principles of communalism are not given correlated expression, class cleavages will arise, which are connected with economic disparities and thereby with political inequalities. Socialism, therefore, can be, and is, the defence of the principles of communalism in a modern setting; it is a form of social organisation that, guided by the principles underlying communism, adopts procedures and measures made necessary by demographic and technological developments. Only under socialism can we reliably accumulate the capital we need for our development and also ensure that the gains of investment are applied for the general welfare.

Socialism is not spontaneous. It does not arise by itself. It has abiding principles according to which the major means of production and distribution ought to be socialised if exploitation of the many by the few is to be prevented; if, that is to say, egalitarianism in the economy is to be protected. Socialist countries in Africa may differ in this or that detail of their policies, but such differences themselves ought not to be arbitrary or subject to vagaries of taste. They must be scientifically explained, as necessities arising from differences in the particular circumstances of the countries themselves.

There is only one way of achieving socialism: by the devising of policies aimed at the general socialist goals, each of which takes its particular form from the specific circumstances of a particular state at a definite historical period. Socialism depends on dialectical and historical materialism, upon the view that there is only one nature subject in all its manifestations to natural laws and that human society is, in this sense, part of nature and subject to its own laws of development.

It is the elimination of fancifulness from socialist action that makes socialism scientific. To suppose that there are tribal, national, or racial socialisms is to abandon objectivity in favour of chauvinism.